Managing Conflict

A Woman's Guide to Controlling Confrontation

CONFLICT EXTINGUISHER

Managing Conflict

A Woman's Guide to Controlling Confrontation

by Deborah Shouse

SkillPath Publications

Editor: Bill Cowles

Layout and cover design: Jason Sprenger

ISBN: 978-1-934589-01-4

10 9 8 7 6 5 4 3 2 07 08 09 10

Printed in the United States of America

Acknowledgements

Thanks to Sarah H. Shouse, M.A., Ph.D. Candidate for consulting on this book and for helping with the psychological context.

Thanks to my life partner Ron Zoglin for his careful reading and excellent suggestions. Susan Fenner, Ph.D. helped me with the outline for the book and always is a font of wonderful ideas.

Other people who added their wisdom, insights and ideas include: Lucille Lowe, Barbara Bartocci, Andrea Warren, Hilee Shouse, Dan Barnett, Robin Silverman, Ginny Job, Maril Crabtree, Sarah Grace Parlak, Danyelle Beaudry-Jones, Jacque Ensign, Carolyn Hall, Bev Cortiana, Barb Friedman, Linda Rodriguez, Jane Wood and Carol Schultz.

Table of Contents

Foreword

It starts in childhood—your little brother wants to sit in the front seat and it's your turn. Your mother insists that you eat all your squash and you hate squash. You want to go to the party with your friends and your parents won't let you go.

Every day there's a voicing of opinions, a difference of perspectives and a clash of wills. That clash can be brief and harmless, with a quick and simple solution: "Take turns sitting in the front seat." Or it can escalate into a rift or a battle of wills: "If I hear one more word about that party, you'll be grounded for a week!"

Now, of course, you are a grown woman and you can eat what you want and go to any party you're invited to. But even though you're independent, sophisticated and mature, those clashes of opinions still spring up all around you. Some are harmless, simply a matter of easy clarification or compromise, and others somehow escalate into full-fledged confrontations.

This is a book about understanding, managing and benefiting from the conflicts in your life—especially those that occur in the workplace. We'll discuss issues such as:

- How does a situation move from a simple conversation to a confrontation?
- Are there certain people who seem to create conflict wherever they go?
- Why are they picking on you?
- What is your role in the conflict?
- How can you take care of yourself without harming or being mean to the other person?
- How do you find the solutions and emerge from the fray a hero?

You'll learn how conflict impacts you, your personality and your work life. You'll find tips, exercises and ideas that will help you understand more about yourself and the kinds of conflicts that most impact you. You'll also explore your own natural conflict persona and discover ideas that can help deflect or minimize conflicts.

Throughout the book, we use six acronyms to describe the methods and strategies you can use to defuse conflict and turn it to your own advantage: CONFLICT, STILL, THERE, REST, CHILL and CALM.

This book will improve and inspire your confidence in your own unique problem-solving skills when you:

1. Read it through first
2. Go back and complete the exercises
3. Apply the techniques illustrated by the six acronyms

Here's to your success!

CONFLICT EXTINGUISHER

Chapter One

Conflict as Communications: The Enriching Benefits of Conflict

Conflict is normal

When people say, "Vive la difference!" they might as well be saying, "Vive la conflict."

Consider these three examples of "differences":

- *Shirley liked to talk directly to the point. She did not appreciate niceties and abhorred small talk. She believed a manager should dole out assignments and save the chatting for after work. Her administrative assistant Callie, however, treasured her personal connections with people. She believed getting to know someone was part of doing her job well.*
- *Margo just wanted to get through the day. She needed this job to pay for her son's special schooling and she wanted to do her work and go right home. Her co-worker Eileen's career was just starting and she was working hard to advance in this company. Her work was the center of her life and she took every deadline, every assignment, very seriously.*
- *Patty was an optimist. When someone talked, she listened for the bright side. When someone gave her news, she focused on what was going well. Patty's project supervisor, Tamara, liked to face the worst-case scenario first. She considered the negative before she moved forward. She always heard the bad news and always worried about the things that needed fixing.*

These three simple scenarios feature six smart, interesting and hard-working women who have a variety of differences that are ripe for conflict. The causes of the conflict could be:

- Miscommunication
- Different perceptions
- Emotional disconnects, such as not feeling valued
- Different personality styles
- Different goals

From your own workplace experiences, name some other causes of conflict:

1. ____________________
2. ____________________
3. ____________________
4. ____________________

The creativity of clashing

Emmy was concerned about her new job in the accounting department of a big company. Everyone acted quite pleasant, but she felt an underlying tension. When she asked a co-worker about the sense of tension she felt, he told her, "Our boss doesn't like to deal with conflict. She won't tolerate any kind of confrontation. In fact, she's even stopped our weekly meetings. As a result, there are a lot of unspoken frustrations."

Over the next weeks, Emmy heard some of these frustrations. They seemed like no big deal to her—issues that they would have easily resolved at her old job. But here, the tension continued to build.

By refusing to acknowledge conflict, Emmy's boss was fueling the tension. She was missing out on a chance to develop clear communications standards, expand the department's way of thinking and build a connective, caring work environment. Over a period of time, the unvoiced frustrations, irritations and anger that permeated the office could erupt into serious confrontations.

Conflict is an opportunity to listen to someone you don't agree with. That means you have the possibility of widening your thinking and incorporating another point of view. You also have the possibility of clarifying your own values and priorities, separating them from any emotional baggage, and clearly expressing yourself to another person. Healthy conflict breeds healthy communication. For many women, such self-advocacy and self-expression inspires and fuels their personal growth.

What has conflict done for you lately?

Jessica finally spoke out about her boss's unfair treatment. He was always yelling at her to hurry projects along and he was constantly interrupting her so she couldn't concentrate. For weeks, she stifled her irritation. When she finally spoke up, the results surprised her. Here's her report:

- What was the nature of conflict? *Productivity at work. Work environment. Communications.*
- Who was it with? *My boss.*
- What did you do about it? *I spoke out my frustration. I told him I was normally an on-time worker, but both his interruptions and his yelling rattled me so much it was hard to concentrate and produce.*
- What were the positive results? *He actually stood still and listened. He said, "I don't yell. I don't interrupt. I just offer suggestions." I was then able to tell him that those "suggestions" were harming my productivity. I asked if we could schedule a time every week for suggestions. He agreed.*
- What did you learn or do differently? *I learned my boss is capable of listening. I learned he didn't understand his own behavior. I am going to speak up much sooner when something bothers me.*

Think about the times that conflict has forced you to come to a decision, clarify your values or speak up, either for yourself or someone else. Think about the times that conflict has brought you closer to an individual, group or yourself.

List three conflicts from any part of your life that have positively impacted you:

Conflict 1: ______________________________

- What was the nature of conflict? ____________________
- Who was it with? ____________________
- What did you do about it? ____________________
- What were the positive results? ____________________
- What did you learn or do differently? ____________________

Conflict 2: ______________________________

- What was the nature of conflict? ____________________
- Who was it with? ____________________
- What did you do about it? ____________________
- What were the positive results? ____________________
- What did you learn or do differently? ____________________

Conflict 3: ______________________________

- What was the nature of conflict? ____________________
- Who was it with? ____________________
- What did you do about it? ____________________
- What were the positive results? ____________________
- What did you learn or do differently? ____________________

Now look at the three examples and ask yourself:

- Are they focused on the same issues?
- Are they with the same person or with a certain personality type?
- Are they with an authority figure, an employee or a co-worker?
- Are they at a certain time of day or at a certain setting?

Finally, list the things these conflicts have in common. This will help you understand more about your own role in conflict and understand the types of situations that are tense for you:

Conflict 1: ____

____

____

Conflict 2: ____

____

____

Conflict 3: ____

____

____

Conflict Quenchers

Conflict-proofing tips

Now that you know the whos, whats and whens of your primary types of conflicts, see what you can do to head off conflict situations. Here are three ideas:

1. The yum factor: An apple a day keeps the conflict at bay

Sarah can get quite grouchy when she's tired or hungry. She keeps a stash of healthy treats in a small refrigerator in her office. An afternoon snack helps her keep her blood sugar boosted, so she doesn't get worn out and take things too personally or snap at someone. She also shares those treats with whoever comes in. She has discovered that food fuels fondness and reduces potential frictions.

- The great news is—food can help reduce the chances of conflict! Keep a stash of healthy treats in your office. Nurture and nourish yourself during those times when you feel tired and hungry and are prone to snap.

2. Center stage: Keep calm to the core

Every time she's around David, Alison feels like biting his head off. His whiny voice, his accusatory manner, the pompous way he talks on and on without listening drive her crazy.

But she has learned the hard way that biting his head off really does no good—he'll grow another head without missing a word. Whenever she's going to be around David, Alison makes sure she has a few minutes to center herself. She reminds herself that the accusations David makes are not personal. She reminds herself she does not have to react—she has the inner strength to remain silent when she needs to.

- Most conflicts are small and petty. They have nothing to do with you and what your goals and priorities are. Before you go near a tense situation, get centered. Take three deep breaths. Remember your larger, higher self. Read an inspirational quote, one that inspires you to be your best. Remind yourself that this person, this issue, is only a small part of your magnificent life.

3. Habits: Form before the storm

Never waste a moment, Adele's mother always told her. Which is why Adele was always either on time to the minute or she was less than five minutes late.

"No meeting ever starts on time," Adele figured. "Getting there early is a waste of valuable time."

Her co-worker, Leticia, thought differently. She was taught to show up ten minutes early. "You never know what will happen when you're early," her mother told her. "Plus, it's a sign of respect for the meeting planner."

Leticia was irritated by the cavalier way Adele strolled into a meeting right as it began. She didn't understand why Adele was so disrespectful. Adele couldn't believe how irresponsible Leticia was, hanging out in the meeting room with nothing going on. Didn't she have work to do?

- Differing values and perceptions can cause discomfort and conflict. So often, no one is technically "wrong" but both people are irritated. When you find yourself irritated, ask some questions to see if you can understand why the person behaves in that way. There's often wisdom on both sides and a wise meeting place in the middle.

In this chapter ...

Conflict as teacher and connector

This **CONFLICT** acronym includes the components of good problem solving and conflict deflection.

You'll see it at the end of each chapter, showing you the types of tools you have used in learning about those aspects of conflict management. You can also use this **CONFLICT** connector as a reference guide before entering into any conflicted or problem-solving situation.

When you successfully handle a conflict situation, you:

C Concentrate on the facts, rather than the emotions

O Open yourself to opportunity for growth and learning

N Notice how others view life

F Form new ways of looking at a situation

L Learn deeper listening levels

I Incorporate your priorities and values along with your analytical skills

C Connect through problem solving

T Target solutions that invite creativity and build community

Chapter Two

Your Conflict Continuum: Learning From the Inside Out

Have you ever caught yourself in a movie theater, mentally shouting at the hero to turn back, quick, and just talk to his girlfriend? It's often much easier to look at another person's life, see their conflicts and figure out ways they could solve them. To improve your own conflict quotient, it's important to understand your inner conflicts and how they influence your outer life.

Backstage jitters: The inner conflict

Even when we're not interacting with other people, most of us have enough inner conflict to fuel many mini-melodramas. When an outer conflict triggers the inner voices, you're more likely to explode than explore. When someone pushes one of your "hot" buttons, it can take a while to separate your fired-up emotions from the cool, hard facts. The more you know about your own inner conflicts, the more objectively and compassionately you'll be able to analyze outer conflicts.

Keri walked into the office and instantly that knot returned to her stomach. Despite the pep talk she gave herself early this morning, despite the soothing music she listened to on the way to work, she could already feel the tension. And she hadn't even seen Val yet.

Yesterday, when Val attacked Keri's marketing plan right in the middle of Keri's presentation, she almost cried. The knot grew larger as Keri thought about the strategic planning meeting today.

Keri had no idea how Val would act. And how she would react. Trying to avoid a potential contact with Val, Keri raced straight to her office without even saying her usual hellos to the administrative staff. Now they would probably think she was snubbing them. Now they would probably get angry at her too.

Keri's friend Francine did not understand Keri's behavior at all. "Aren't you angry? Don't you want to speak up for yourself?" Francine asked Keri during their coffee break.

But Keri just shook her head. Despite her education and experience, her self-esteem was near zero. By attacking her marketing plan, Val had tapped one of Keri's inner conflicts—"Am I good enough? Can I do this job? Will people look at me and see I am worthless and faking it?"

Francine's inner warriors were from a different army. "How can I stick up for myself and not be perceived as wimpy?" was one of Francine's enduring inner struggles.

Here are some other typical inner conflicts:

- Should you be spending so much time at work? Should you be spending more time with your family or friends?
- Is this job making the best use of your talents? Would you be better off making less money and doing something that's your passion?
- Are you being yourself at work or are you squashing important parts of your personality to try to fit in?
- Does anyone notice the good work you're doing? Should you be more assertive in talking about your accomplishments or should you wait for someone to notice?
- Are you taking care of yourself? Are you in the right relationship, job, volunteer job, spiritual community, etc?

Other inner conflicts may include fears of not being "enough." You may feel you are not:

- Smart enough
- Assertive enough
- Persistent enough
- Creative enough
- Personable enough

List other "not enoughs" that periodically go through your mind:

As you go through your day, listen for these inner worriers. Make a list of the conflicts and concerns. Notice if they are louder at certain times of the day, e.g., when you're hungry, tired, especially stressed, arriving at work or leaving work.

Here's an example of how to use this technique:

- Inner conflict: *Is this the right job for me?*
- Times you are most concerned about this: *Driving to or from work; at work anytime something goes wrong; anytime you hear about somebody living her passion.*

- Inner conflict: ____________________
  ____
- Times you are most concerned about this: ____________________
  ____
- Inner conflict: ____________________
  ____
- Times you are most concerned about this: ____________________
  ____
- Inner conflict: ____________________
  ____
- Times you are most concerned about this: ____________________
  ____

Soothing the inner worrier

Start by finding ways to soothe your inner conflicts. Analyze each inner worrier and separate the:

- Emotions
- Concerns
- Options
- Action

Sharon joined the marketing department, with a promise that she'd be able to move from behind-the-scenes software development into more client contact and presentations.

But so far her chances to go beyond the computer were less than byte-size. Every time she brought up the subject, her manager nodded and encouraged her to remain patient. She had been patient for two years and she was starting to seethe. Even though the job paid well, she was bored. Plus, she wanted to advance, and she knew her chances for promotion depended on her becoming more visible. She felt trapped and frustrated. Should she stuff her feelings, be grateful for her steady income and remain patient? Should she go to her boss's boss? Should she forget about stability and seek out another company?

These worry warriors invaded her mind every morning as she drove to work, every late afternoon and most evenings as she drove home.

When Sharon delved into her own issues, she discovered:

- **Emotions:** Frustration, irritation, anger, worry, fear, fear of not being smart or talented enough
- **Concerns:** What if I'm stuck behind the desk the rest of my life? What if I never get noticed? What if I never get a promotion? What do I really value in life? Am I living out my values?
- **Options:** With the help of a friend, Sharon brainstormed her options. Here are five of the potential options they came up with:
  1. Find a Toastmaster's group to join so Sharon could gain experience speaking.
  2. Brainstorm with the manager's pet presenter. Let her know Sharon's desires and ask for her advice. Ask if she was willing to mentor Sharon.

3. Volunteer to be a co-presenter with one of the marketing people. Agree to make up her own work, so her manager would not think she was shirking her duties.
4. Write down some of her presentation ideas. Share those ideas with her mentor—then ask her to set up a meeting with the manager for the three of them.
5. Share the ideas with her manager and try to get permission to work on one.

- **Action:** Sharon found an early morning Toastmaster group and began going to meetings. She also reached out to the star presenter, to ask if she would advise or mentor her.

There is a feeling of relief at just identifying and acknowledging your emotions and concerns. Listing options is empowering and taking action lessens the inner conflict. Sharon had more confidence she would not abandon her goals of presenting and speaking now that she was actually doing something about it.

Doing this inner conflict exercise makes you less vulnerable to outer conflict and gives you tools to use when working through conflict with others.

What's your story? Understanding your conflict characteristics

In the movies, conflict is essential to a good story—a key to the hero's ability to grow and change. And of course, we all want to grow and change! The more you understand the central conflicts in your life, the more easily you'll be able to manage them.

In most situations, there's an above-ground reason for the conflict ("You don't get to work on time.") and there is an underground reason for the conflict ("You don't respect me.")

Think about the last two conflicts you experienced, large or small. Imagine you are writing a short synopsis of these two "growth" experiences. Answer these questions about each to more fully understand the kinds of inner conflicts you most often face.

Conflict I:

1. Who was the conflict with? (Co-worker, boss, family member, vendor, other)

2. What was the conflict about?

3. Who brought the conflict out into the open? (You, the other person, a neutral party, other)

4. What were the inner conflicts for you?

5. Did your inner conflict get hooked?

6. What were the results of the conflict conversations? (A step forward, a solution reached, a step backward, other)

7. How did you feel after the conversation?

8. What did you do right? ____________________

____

____

9. What could you have done better? ____________________

____

____

10. How did your inner conflict change? ____________________

____

____

Conflict II:

1. Who was the conflict with? (Co-worker, boss, family member, vendor, other) ____________________

____

____

2. What was the conflict about? ____________________

____

____

3. Who brought the conflict out into the open? (You, the other person, a neutral party, other) ____________________

____

____

4. What were the inner conflicts for you? ____________________

____

____

5. Did your inner conflict get hooked? ______________________________________

____

____

6. What were the results of the conflict conversations? (A step forward, a solution reached, a step backward, other) ______________________________________

____

____

7. How did you feel after the conversation? ______________________________________

____

____

8. What did you do right? ______________________________________

____

____

9. What could you have done better? ______________________________________

____

____

10. How did your inner conflict change? ______________________________________

____

____

Now read both conflict scenarios and see if you detect any patterns. Is a certain person pouring conflict into your life? Does a certain work issue plague you? Are there inner triggers or irritants that get you every time? How do you feel about your own responses or reactions?

The more you focus on your conflict readiness and abilities, the more you'll enjoy the show, knowing you're able to deflect and sail through potential conflicts.

Conflict Quenchers

Creating calm

Notice how you feel as you leave the house and journey to work. What inner conflicts surface? Calm them by choosing something soothing and affirming to do on your way to work.

Here are three examples:

- *Virginia listens to her favorite music on the bus. Before she transfers to another bus, she dashes into a coffee shop and buys a luxurious cup of cappuccino, to remind herself she is worth it.*
- *Andrea has posted affirmations on her rear view mirror and on her dashboard, affirming she has everything she needs to have a calm and productive day at work.*
- *Cynthia reads inspirational quotes and poetry in her carpool. She pauses before she enters the office and reminds herself she has enough time to get everything done.*

Fizzling friction

Create a small "friction-fizzling" ritual before you go into your office. Pick something that gives you inner calm and strength and addresses your inner conflicts. Your ritual can be quite simple: As you put your briefcase or purse on your desk, remind yourself you are smart and interesting and have everything you need.

Whether your friction fizzler is a soothing song, a comforting cappuccino or an uplifting affirmation, this small action reminds you to stay calm, even when conflict is swirling around you.

In this chapter . . .

To understand more about your own inner conflicts, you have been:

- **C** **Concentrating on the facts, rather than the emotions**
- **O** **Opening yourself to opportunity for growth and learning**
- **N** **Noticing how others view life**
- **F** Forming new ways of looking at a situation
- **L** Learning deeper listening levels
- **I** Incorporating your priorities and values along with your analytical skills
- **C** Connecting through problem solving
- **T** Targeting solutions that invite creativity and build community

Chapter Three

Putting Together the Personality Puzzle: The Conflict Persona

Personalities can get in the way of even the most practiced problem-solvers. The solution is to learn as much about yourself—and about the people around you—as you can.

Home-grown conflict personas

Most people have had informal "home-schooling" in conflict resolution. The way our family dealt with conflict often makes an impact on how we deal with conflict. But what worked for us as children may be out of place or ineffective at work. When we understand our initial reactions to conflict, we can select behaviors that are still appropriate and try to avoid behaviors that are not. Here are some examples:

Reconnecting the isolator

Marge grew up in an explosive family. Her father was an angry man, randomly raging and throwing things. Her mother yelled back. Her older sister tried to smooth things over. Her brother tried to avoid the conflict by drinking, taking drugs and stealing. Marge tried to disappear into the woodwork and stay out of the chaos.

When conflicts flared up at work, Marge felt a clenching in her stomach and a tightening in her throat. Her first instinct was to go into her office and lock the door. But since Marge was a manager, she almost always had to get involved in solving the conflict.

"Of course, the work conflicts are much different than what I went through at home," Marge said. "But still, there's that instant when I feel like a helpless girl again. I take a few minutes to remind myself of who I am now and how strong I am. I remind myself, we are all adults. No one can harm me. Once I do that, I'm pretty good at staying calm in conflict. After all, I've had lots of previous experience."

Relaxing the pleaser

Helen grew up with parents who had opposite conflict styles. Her mother liked to get in there and talk things through, then move on. Her father simply retreated into his own world, sulking and giving everyone the silent treatment. Helen's older sister ignored the whole thing but Helen tried to coax her father out of his shell. She listened to her mother tell her side of the story. She tried to get the two of them together and talking. She always felt the fight was her fault and she tried to be extra good and nice so the arguing would end.

Helen tried to use these pleasing abilities in the workplace. At the slightest hint of friction, Helen was soothing people, trying to defuse any tension. But often, by inserting herself in the middle of an issue, Helen just delayed resolution or prolonged problems.

Helen got feedback from friends, co-workers and a counselor who helped her curb her instincts. When she felt this burning desire to please, Helen learned to stop and ask herself: "Does this issue really concern me? Am I a part of this problem or am I merely a bystander?"

When the answer to the first question was no, which it often was, Helen trained herself to step away from the quarrel. "Of course, I knew that conflicts could be healthy, but my pleasing instincts were so ingrained that it took me several years to notice how I was often making things worse," Helen said.

Becoming above-board with the manipulator

"My mother was in charge of our household," Sandy says. But her passive-aggressive father constantly undermined his wife. Sandy spent her childhood noticing how easily a manipulative man could undermine a strong woman. Sandy did not want to be undermined. Like her father, she shied away from direct confrontation, preferring to get her way through underground behaviors.

When Sandy brought her manipulative skills into the workplace, there was instant trouble. Co-workers complained. Bosses demoted her. "I thought I was just doing what everyone else was doing—trying to get my way," Sandy said.

When Sandy went to counseling and took a class on anger management, she began to understand how disruptive her conflict style was. Whenever she felt like undermining an agreement, she stopped and asked herself, "What am I thinking right now? What am I feeling right now? What are my fears? What do I need to do to feel safe and comfortable?" Once she identified her thoughts and feelings, she could sort through them and decide if they were related to the current conflict.

"When I remember to express myself, I am usually satisfied with the results," Sandy reported. "And being direct is much less work!"

Backing off the director

Wendy grew up with her grandmother, her single mom and three little sisters. Her grandmother was indifferent and her mother was indecisive. Wendy became the director of the family. She learned to quickly analyze a situation, come up with a solution, tell people what she expected from them and move on. Her directness kept her family going and lent a much-needed structure to their household.

When Wendy went into the workplace, she found whole groups of people who felt they could solve their own issues without any direction from her.

"I was so proud of my instant ability to size up situations and come up with solutions," Wendy said. "But that rarely worked around co-workers. People thought I was bossy and aggressive. I had to tone down and modify those skills and let others solve their own problems."

Home-grown conflict experiences: A basis for your current style

You have your own stories of personal conflict resolution. As you analyze your conflict style, think of your growing-up experiences. Answer these questions about the people who impacted you:

1. What kinds of issues did your parents argue/fight about?
2. What was each person's style?
    - Mother's style:
    - Father's style:
3. What role did you play in your family? (e.g., pleaser, bad girl, historian, isolator)
4. What kinds of conflicts did you get into with your parents or guardians?
5. How did they want you to express yourself?
6. How did you express yourself?
7. What did you learn about conflict from your growing-up experiences?
8. Which of those lessons work for you now?
9. Which of those lessons don't help you and your relationships?

Most of us can look at our own backgrounds and see a variety of ways of reacting to conflict. If we understand our own patterns, then we're better able to deal with conflict and to avoid automatic responses. As we observe others, we can also notice their patterns. That gives us useful information in avoiding or smoothing conflicts with them.

There are dozens of conflict personas. See how many of these styles you recognize:

- **The Innocent:** Proclaims, "It's not my fault"
- **The Silent:** Withdraws and refuses to discuss the issue
- **The Attacker:** Defends herself and attacks you, before the words are out of your mouth
- **The Instigator:** Loves to stir up tensions and cook up conflict
- **The Analyzer:** Likes to analyze every aspect of the conflict in excruciating detail
- **The Historian:** Remembers every argument you've ever had and loves to bring up each one
- **The Listener:** Asks questions and actively listens to answers
- **The Isolator:** Likes to hide and pretend nothing is wrong
- **The Fixer:** Rushes in to fix any conflict
- **The Pleaser:** Uses niceness to try to defuse tension
- **The Joker:** Deflects conflict by trying to be funny
- **The Involver:** Gets other people involved in the issue

Add your own:

- **The** ______________________________
- **The** ______________________________
- **The** ______________________________

What personality styles are you most familiar with?

What styles are you most comfortable with?

What styles irritate you the most?

What is your conflict style?

To learn more about your own style of conflict crunching, fill in these blanks:

When a conflict arises, my first instinct is to ______________________________(Write down an action or actions; e.g., get involved, run, attack.)

When a conflict arises, I feel __________________________ (Write down emotions; e.g., scared, excited, worried.)

When a conflict arises, I try to___________________________ (Write down an action; e.g., take a deep breath, sit and listen, separate my emotions.)

My conflict-solving skills include (Name some of the skills you feel make you good at dealing with conflicts.):

1. ____

2. ____

3. ____

4. ____

The areas I'd like to improve include:

1. ____

2. ____

3. ____

4. ____

Understanding your conflict quotient: Exploring your conflict persona

Different situations and different people bring out different aspects of our conflict personas. Some personality types grate on us while others soothe us. Some tense situations bring out our righteous anger while other tense situations don't faze us. See which of your conflict personas each of these situations brings out.

1. During a coffee break, you hear someone from another department make a disparaging and untrue remark about a friend from your department. What do you do? Choose the answer that feels the most comfortable for you:

    a. Ignore the remark. Figure it's not your problem.

    b. Confront the person in front of everyone there. Tell them they are wrong and you resent them spreading untruths.

    c. Find the person alone in their office and ask to hear what they are feeling and thinking. Listen carefully, then tell them how the remark made you feel and any action you recommend.

    d. Make a list of all the things that irritate you about the person who made the remark. Be prepared to list her wrongdoings if she says anything about your friend again.

    e. Other ____

    ____

2. As a manager, you have an employee who is literally falling asleep on the job. This person has even fallen asleep during a meeting! This unauthorized napping is causing unrest with the other employees. You need to talk to this employee. Which feels most comfortable to you?

    a. Forget it. At least he's quiet. Be grateful he's not arguing about the new sales quota.

    b. The next time you catch him napping, give him a written warning and let him know this behavior is unacceptable.

    c. Set up a meeting to talk to him. Ask questions so you can understand the underlying emotional and physical reasons for the problem.

d. Look through his file for past mistakes. Be prepared to talk about his problems with computer training two years ago.

e. Other ____

____

3. Your boss is piling on the work. You feel overwhelmed, underappreciated and stressed out. The moment you even begin to feel caught up, there's another project dumped on your desk. What is your plan?

   a. Just keep on working. Eventually you will get caught up. Or you'll get used to being behind.

   b. March into his office with the three most current undone projects. Tell your boss you'll need an assistant to complete this work.

   c. The next time he comes into your office, ask him to prioritize the tasks for you. Tell him you want to do a good job for him and don't know how to do so, with so much undone work piling up. Ask him to tell you why there's so much work.

   d. Forget your boss and complain to his boss. You have unfinished projects from months ago.

   e. Other ____

   ____

Match your responses to the conflict persona types listed below. Are they the same in each situation? What other personas did you select?

A = Isolator

B = Director

C = Listener

D = Historian

What do you see as the advantages and disadvantages of the conflict personas you chose in each situation?

1. ______________________________

____

2. ______________________________

____

3. ______________________________

____

Understanding the irritation factor

Some people don't even notice these kinds of behaviors. Other people find them aggravating:

- *Emily always carries a wadded-up tissue in her hand.*
- *Josh always says "How's it going, kid?" when he sees you.*
- *Bill has a story, a long story, for every situation under the sun.*
- *Karen starts every other sentence, "Well of course, you know better, but what I think is..."*

Most of us can't help it—certain types of personalities or behaviors tend to rankle us. Maybe these personalities mirror a part of ourselves we don't appreciate. Maybe they remind us of someone we'd rather forget. They may take us back to a situation where we had no control. Perhaps one person talks in a way we find grating. Another person has mannerisms and behaviors that set us on edge. The more we understand about the triggers and sources of our own irritants, the more we can separate the person from the problem.

The irritation itinerary: An exploration

For one day, keep an irritation diary. Think about:

The person …

- Who is irritating you?
- What is your relationship with them?
- What type of persona are they?

The situation …

- What is the basic situation?

The trigger …

- What did he or she say? List any words or phrases that particularly get to you.
- What did he or she do? List any actions or types of behaviors that make you want to shout!

Your feelings …

- How did you feel after the irritation?

Your action …

- What did you do?
- What did you want to do?

Your associations, your history …

- What did the person or the situation remind you of, if anything?

Your options …

- Is there another way to look at or interpret the situation or behavior?

At the end of the day, review your notes. Do you see any patterns? What ideas do you have to reduce your feelings or irritation? Share with a trusted co-worker and get their input.

As long as you are analyzing irritants, can you think of behaviors or phrases or anything else you might do that would irritate certain people?

Write down your potentially irritating habits and see if you want to make any changes:

My behaviors: ____

____

____

My words or phrases: ____

____

____

Conflict personas coming to life

Alison just hopes the new boss realizes what is going on. At the last three meetings, Gary has criticized her and her department, accusing them of not meeting deadlines and not working hard enough. Alison did not want to get into an argument in front of the new boss. She also does not want her department's reputation sullied and maligned.

"That Gary sure has it in for you," Peggy, her administrative assistant, says during their team lunch break.

"He just has it in for someone and I happen to fill that role right now," Alison tells Peggy. Alison has seen Gary do the same thing to the woman she replaced. That woman transferred out of their department. Alison has no intention of transferring, but she also doesn't know the best way to handle Gary.

If you were mentoring Alison:

- What advice would you give her?
- What kinds of questions would you have her ask herself?
- What kind of support would you suggest?
- What kind of conflict persona does Gary have?
- What about Alison—what is your guess about her conflict profile?
- What would be her next steps?

Conflict Quenchers

Quiet on the set

Have fun analyzing conflict personas in the movies. Select a movie you like and analyze the conflict styles. What kind of movie would it be if everyone was a clear communicator and understood her own conflict style?

Return to the comfort

Just as you've been exploring the sources of your conflict orientation, now explore the things that give you comfort. Make a list of things that you can do to make yourself feel nurtured or special. On days that are full of stress, do at least one of those nurturing things for yourself.

For example, Susan loves fresh flowers. Every Monday, she stops at the grocery store on her way into the office and buys an inexpensive bouquet. Just looking at the flowers calms her.

Fragrant teas calm Mai. She keeps a collection of tea tins in her office and a few tea cups. When she needs to feel soothed, she can simply add hot water to a favorite cup and steep in the warmth and aroma.

In this chapter . . .

You have learned more about your conflict persona by:

- **C** Concentrating on the facts, rather than the emotions
- **O** **Opening yourself to opportunity for growth and learning**
- **N** **Noticing how others view life**
- **F** **Forming new ways of looking at a situation**
- **L** Learning deeper listening levels
- **I** Incorporating your priorities and values along with your analytical skills
- **C** Connecting through problem solving
- **T** Targeting solutions that invite creativity and build community

Chapter Four

From Clash to Crash: The Early Warning Who, What, Where and When of Friction

As you drive down the highway, signs constantly alert you to the road conditions ahead:

- Danger: Falling rocks
- Warning: Slippery when wet
- Caution: Road work and detour ahead
- Be prepared to stop
- Yield to oncoming traffic
- Do not trespass

Wouldn't it reduce stress if you could introduce such alerts into the workplace? Imagine walking through the office and seeing the various signs on people's doors:

- Danger: Inner conflict alert—fought with spouse
- Warning: Erupts when criticized
- Caution: Grouchy and argumentative when tired and hungry
- Be prepared to stop and listen to what I have to say
- Yield to oncoming ideas
- Do not trespass

Put them on alert: Make a list of five signs you'd like to have for your cubicle or office:

1. ______________________________
2. ______________________________
3. ______________________________
4. ______________________________
5. ______________________________

Stop, look and listen before crossing

"Stay on the path," the sign in the national park demands. The plain dirt-packed path winds through gorgeous land. You would like to get closer to the lush looking trees. You would like to tiptoe off the path to better see the moose grazing in the distance. But the ranger warned you—the earth's crust may be thin in places, barely covering "hot pots" of scalding water. You could sink in deep and be burned in the process.

Conflict is much like straying off the path. You encounter an upset person, turn a different direction, say a wrong word, and you may suddenly find yourself sinking in deep. How do you notice the warning signs that will keep your connected, communicating and relatively conflict-free?

The grade school crossing guard had some sage advice that applies in such situations: Stop. Look. Listen.

Here's an example:

Carolyn and Jeff were walking to a meeting. They passed Donna, a co-worker from marketing, and Carolyn said, "Hey, Donna, how are you?"

"I'm fine," Donna answered. "I'm just fine."

"Wonder what's wrong with her," Carolyn said.

"What do you mean?" Jeff said. "She just said she was fine."

Carolyn looked at Jeff. "Yes, but did you hear the way she said it? Something is wrong; I could hear it in her voice. She sounded like she's upset."

The meeting room was half empty and Carolyn and Jeff stopped to get a cup of coffee. As she surveyed the conference table, Carolyn said, "Boy, Sandra must have had a great month."

"Really?" Jeff said. "How do you know?"

"Look where she's sitting, right near the head of the table. Usually, she's scrunched down at the end. She must feel pretty good about herself."

Carolyn and Jeff took seats in the middle of the table. Five minutes after the meeting was scheduled to start, their boss, Evelyn, walked in, her ever-present headset on. She clutched a stack of folders to her chest and continued her cell phone conversation as she used her foot to pull out the chair at the head of the table.

"She's looking for someone to dump on," Carolyn whispered to Jeff. "Listen to the clipped way she's speaking. It sounds like she wants to bite that person's head off. I hope she doesn't bite ours off."

Evelyn finished her call, crossed her arms and said tersely, "OK, everyone. Let's get started. We have no time to waste."

The meeting went downhill from there. Evelyn rattled off changes in quotas and informed them, "Things will be different." She would make sure they emerged from the sales slump that had plagued them for the last three months. Then she praised Sandra as the only associate who was fulfilling her potential. Jeff and Carolyn exchanged looks. Several people coughed and shifted in their chairs.

After the meeting, Jeff said to Carolyn, "You were right about Evelyn. You were right about Sandra. Now I'm waiting to find out what's bothering Donna. How did you know those things?"

Carolyn was an expert at the stop, look and listen method of detecting and hopefully deflecting conflict. She was constantly looking at facial expressions, body language and positioning. She was listening for tone of voice, word choice, inflection and volume. Carolyn could sense who was ripe for conflict.

Discovering the clues: The early warning signs of conflict

Some of the signs and breeding grounds for conflict include:

- **Change!** Any change, good or bad, large or small, can make people feel insecure and uncomfortable.
- **Differences.** Natural differences in personality, values, priorities, cultural background, communications style, management style and more may cause friction.
- **Misunderstood communications.** What you say is not always what someone else hears. What you mean when you write an e-mail is not always what someone else reads.
- **Lack of important information.** People can feel stressed and upset when they don't have enough information to understand or analyze a situation.
- **Lack of listening skills.** Low-level listening is the cause of numerous conflicts.
- **Inner conflicts that leak out.** When inner issues are triggered by outer stimuli, it can lead to increased tension and conflict.
- **Personal insecurities** and situations that threaten those insecurities. Take away our titles, the jobs we do best, our peer group—and most of us feel threatened and ready to fight.
- **Territoriality.** When people feel someone has trespassed on their project, ideas, workspace, clients, employees or more, they may want to defend their territory.

What other issues create conflict at your workplace?

1. ______________________________

2. ______________________________

3. ______________________________

4. ______________________________

What types of conflict issues most often get to you?

1. ______________________________

2. ______________________________

3. ______________________________

In your own workplace, where are the areas of potential conflict this month? What is changing and where are communications murky?

Carolyn's list might look like this:

- **Change**—Evelyn is changing the quotas and telling them "Things will be different." Sandra has changed seats. (This could be a good change but it still causes a feeling of tension.) Something has changed with Donna and Carolyn is not sure what.
- **Lack of important information.** Evelyn is not telling them how things will be different. This breeds conflict as everyone nervously creates their own personalized interpretation.
- **Misunderstood communication.** Praising Sandra alone while neglecting the others makes for a dissatisfied team. Some people are hearing, "You are not worthwhile. You are not doing your job." Carolyn can imagine the inter-office e-mails and phone calls that will erupt after the meeting.
- **Lack of listening skills.** Even Carolyn, who prides herself on listening well, faded off because Evelyn talked so long and so fast and was so accusatory. Carolyn is guessing that each person heard something different and that no one knows clearly what to do.

Lights, camera and observation: Becoming a conflict detector

Like Carolyn, you can learn to spot potential conflict situations. Pick a day that's packed with meetings and interactions. Then put yourself behind an imaginary camera and look at the big picture.

From your objective perspective, you can better separate the emotions from the issues and reduce your chances of getting caught up in a personality-driven conflict.

Use a wide angle lens and notice the drama. See the gestures and body language—the folding of arms across the chest that might indicate a closed mind (but remember, it could also indicate a cold room); the wide stance that could indicate a feeling of power; fidgeting, which could indicate nervousness. Go for a close-up and focus on the facial expressions. Look for any signs of exasperation, frustration and superiority—the rolling of eyes, the subtle shaking of the head, the angling of the body away from the person talking, the smirk. Notice how people are positioned around the table or the room and who is sitting near whom.

Now tune into the sounds in the room. Listen for tone of voice, use of language. Listen for words that indicate anger or frustration—should, can't believe, always, never. Look for language that indicates competition rather than collaboration, such as "I know" versus "I believe." Look for changes in behaviors and changes in routines.

As you analyze, take into consideration the circumstances, personality type, cultural background and other factors that might inspire the behavior.

Now look at yourself. What kinds of clues are you giving? What would you notice if you took an objective look at yourself, your body language, your tone and words? Are there unconscious things you do that might attract or ignite conflict?

Your body language …

1. ______________________________

2. ______________________________

3. ______________________________

Your tone and word choice …

1. ______________________________

2. ______________________________

3. ______________________________

Other clues …

1. ______________________________

2. ______________________________

3. ______________________________

The way people use words makes a big difference in soothing or stirring conflict.

Look at the difference in these sentences. Presumably, each pair has the same meaning, but they have a very different connotation:

- "That's what you think!"
- "I'm happy to know your thoughts."
- "If only you hadn't done, said … "
- "I'd be curious to know what your strategy was when you said … "
- "Forget it!"
- "Why don't we discuss options?"

Exercise: Hidden meanings

Think back to the last time you shared childhood stories with friends or siblings. As you reminisce about the same event, notice the many versions and interpretations of the story. Be aware of the mud beneath the flowers. Often, each person has her or his own take on what happened, influenced by inner voices, mood, personality and more.

Here's an exercise designed to help you hone your conflict detectors. Remember how Carolyn was quick to pick up on something in Donna's tone in her "I'm fine. I'm just fine." Practice imagining moods, personalities and situations that would cause someone's benign answer to the "How are you?" question to be fraught with extra meaning.

With a partner, repeat these simple phrases, implying as many different meanings as possible. You've been part of this question-and-answer ritual many times. Start with the casual approach as a way of acknowledging each other's presence:

- Partner I: "How are you?"
- Partner II: "I'm fine, just fine."

Here are some other ideas:

- Imagine someone innocently asking the question and the other person is irritated and answers sarcastically.
- One person may ask the question in a slow, emotional way, really wanting to know. "How ARE you?" The other may answer in a mournful or resigned way.

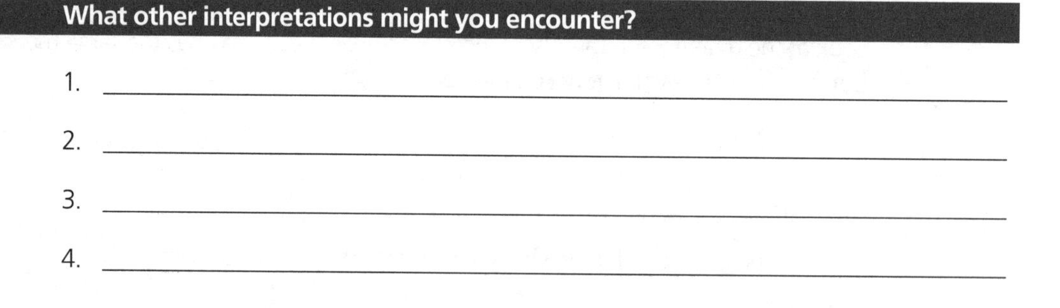

What other interpretations might you encounter?

1. ______________________________
2. ______________________________
3. ______________________________
4. ______________________________

Change on the range: Conflict between parties

At first, Darcy was mildly irritated. She had tried to do her department a favor by stepping in to orchestrate the December holiday party. Lois had been in charge for 10 years and most people were content with the gatherings. But only two months before the event, Lois was transferred and no one wanted to take up the party. So Darcy stepped up. Visions of sugarplums danced in her head as she envisioned the kudos and praise she would receive from her colleagues and her boss for her selfless act. Plus, she liked planning parties. She figured she would put together a team and they would get it done.

But the sugar plums soon turned to prunes when Darcy learned that Lois had not reserved their usual space.

Darcy and her team were forced to find another location and it cost more money. Money they did not have.

Last year the food was catered. They had an open bar and wonderful entertainment. This year, Darcy figured they'd better do a potluck, so they'd have enough money. When she e-mailed everyone, letting them know the new location and inviting them to bring favorite holiday foods, the conflict began. E-mails poured in, wondering why she was undermining Lois, changing their traditions, cheating them out of their holiday feast. Suddenly, Darcy was no hero—she was a villain of the highest order—the Grinch who was trying to steal their holiday.

It's fascinating how a simple change can grow into a conflict—without any bad intentions, desire for self-importance or underhandedness. It wasn't personal and it wasn't anyone's fault. Yet things quickly grew heated.

Darcy did not want to criticize Lois and hoped she would not need to share the information that Lois had neglected to reserve the hall. Darcy consulted her committee and they decided to:

- Share the inside story
- Ask for advice and involvement
- See if someone had the time to take a survey—would they rather have food than drink, drink than entertainment?

Like many holiday stories, this one has a happy ending. Everyone wanted food and drink—they decided to save money on entertainment and create their own. It turned out they had plenty of talent for a first rate show. Though the venue was too small and the bartender they hired had a surly attitude, the party was a success.

Management asked her to lead the committee again next year. Darcy agreed but decided she wanted to minimize the conflict next year.

What are the ingredients of conflict that fueled this story?

1. Example: Change!
2. ______________________________
3. ______________________________
4. ______________________________
5. ______________________________

What actions could Darcy take next year to reduce the friction?

1. ______________________________
2. ______________________________
3. ______________________________
4. ______________________________
5. ______________________________

Conflict Quenchers

Fantasy Isle—the conflict-free zone

Create a conflict-free tropical island in your work space. This can be as simple as a picture of your family or of a favorite place. Perhaps you have a bright piece of fabric, something you like to touch. Perhaps you have music you appreciate. A small plant or favorite souvenir might cheer you on. When the conflicts start brewing, see how quickly and easily you can calm all your senses and bring yourself back to your own inner tropical island.

Separate tables, please

When you start getting hooked into conflict, imagine sitting your rational self at one table and your emotional self at another. Listen and watch with your rational mind. Know that the conflict is usually not personal—even when it seems to be aimed at you.

To calm your emotions, take some deep breaths. Talk to a friend if you're getting emotionally involved in a conflict. Put yourself back behind the imaginary (or real) camera and gain a little perspective. Take a half-hour break from phone and e-mail. Focus on your work. Practice an easy yoga posture or just stand straight with arms at your sides and your feet firmly grounded.

In this chapter . . .

You learned how to notice the signs of a potential conflict situation by:

- C **Concentrating on the facts, rather than the emotions**
- O Opening yourself to opportunity for growth and learning
- N **Noticing how others view life**
- F **Forming new ways of looking at a situation**
- L **Learning deeper listening levels**
- I Incorporating your priorities and values along with your analytical skills
- C Connecting through problem solving
- T Targeting solutions that invite creativity and build community

Chapter Five

Defusing Conflict With Active Listening: Hear the Real Story Behind the Friction

Donna's consistently long lunches were causing a lot of friction in the marketing department.

As manager, Georgia had mentioned to the group the importance of taking only an hour's lunch. She asked that anyone who needed flextime come talk to her. Donna never approached her, yet she was gone for an hour and a half at least two days a week. This had been going on for three weeks. Others were complaining. A few quietly lengthened their own lunch breaks. The department's usual atmosphere of congeniality was eroding. Productivity was suffering. Georgia could feel the tension the moment she walked into the office. She had planned to talk to Donna sooner, but a new marketing campaign and a sudden out-of-town trip had gotten in her way.

Donna was a key person in the department, managing all the print products. She'd worked there for five years and was organized and efficient. She could also be quick to anger if she felt attacked. Georgia did not want to intimidate, alienate or put Donna on the defensive. Here was her approach.

Georgia dropped by Donna's office at a time she knew Donna would be alone. She sat across from Donna and said, "I want to set up a time for us to talk." Georgia kept her voice calm. She sat still, her hands in her lap, her face friendly. "I want to understand why you've been taking long lunch breaks and I want to resolve that situation."

Donna turned red and her mouth tightened.

Georgia said soothingly, "Do you have 45 minutes this afternoon at 1:00?"

Donna glanced at her scheduler and said, "Yes." Georgia could feel the frost in Donna's voice.

"I'll meet you in my office."

Georgia wanted to set the tone for an active listening meeting. She wanted Donna to feel safe during the conversation and after. She wanted Donna to feel that she, Georgia, was "still there," for her, as her manager and as her ally. She also wanted to remind herself to be **still** when she needed to and to stay **there**, present in the meeting.

This simple **STILL THERE** process helped Georgia set up and conduct the meeting:

- **Solo:** To avoid embarrassment and reduce the possibility of anger or defensiveness, find a time when the person is alone to request a meeting.
- **Topic:** Tell the person the topic of the meeting. This reduces stress and helps eliminate the need for gossip and rumors.
- **Intention:** Let the person know your intention. In this case, Georgia's assertion, "I want to understand" implied a desire for collaboration and problem solving.
- **Length of the meeting:** Let the person know the proposed length of the meeting. In this case, Georgia wanted Donna to feel they had time to talk through the issues and not so much time that Donna would get nervous about getting behind in her work.
- **Location and time:** Choose a place that is neutral and private, where neither will be distracted by telephones, e-mails or the work on their desk. Choose a time that is relatively convenient for both.

That afternoon, Georgia made some notes, so she would stay on track during the conversation. She was impressed when Donna walked in with her own notes.

"You're a great worker and you've been a model employee. I'd like you to tell me what's happening in your life that causes you to need extra time at lunch," Georgia said.

Talking rapidly, Donna told Georgia about her infirm mother-in-law who was staying with her.

Donna's husband didn't want to put his mom in a nursing home. The mother refused to go to day care. Donna's husband worked too far away to check on her, so most days Donna had to drive home, check on her mother-in-law and serve her lunch. Often, her mother-in-law needed extras, and Donna could not get away on time.

Georgia listened carefully. She heard how Donna's voice cracked when she talked about being late. She saw how Donna clenched her hands as she spoke.

When Donna finished, Georgia said, "I'm going to repeat back what I just heard. Tell me if I understood what you said."

Georgia repeated back, "What I just heard you say was that your mother-in-law needs to be checked on at lunch time and you are the one who must do it. Once you get home, she often has extra things she needs and you feel you cannot turn her down."

Donna nodded.

"How come you didn't tell me this when I asked you earlier about your lateness? You said you had to take your mother-in-law to the doctor but you never mentioned this daily obligation."

"You sounded angry," Donna answered. "Some of the girls told me I could get in trouble by asking for special favors. So I hoped my mother-in-law would be more reasonable or my husband would change his work schedule. But that hasn't happened."

Georgia saw the tears pooling in Donna's eyes. Donna's hands trembled and her skin was pale.

Georgia repeated the new information that Donna had just shared and again Donna agreed that she had heard correctly.

"Now I'd like to tell you my position," Georgia said. "You are one of my best workers. When you're gone for 90 minutes, people think I'm playing favorites. They feel dissatisfied. They think they too should have long lunches. As you've probably noticed, the atmosphere in our department has become tense. I was feeling frustrated because I didn't understand your behavior. I need us to come up with a solution."

As she spoke, Georgia could feel the emotional stresses of the last weeks flooding through her. She asked Donna to repeat back what she heard.

"My lateness has made the department tense. You're mad at me and I deserve it. I'm sorry. It's all my fault," Donna said, her voice cracking.

Georgia paused. She could see that Donna was becoming more emotional and she wanted to make sure Donna was calm enough to hear what she said.

"I know you're upset. I see what a stressful time this has been for you. I'm not sure you heard everything I said. Donna, first I said that you're one of my best workers. I said that when you break the rules, people think I'm playing favorites and they feel dissatisfied. I never said that I was mad at you. I said that I felt frustrated. But you've explained your situation; I know we can work out a solution. Now, tell me what you heard me say?"

Donna repeated back every point perfectly. This time, Georgia felt Donna had heard and understood her.

Prior to and during the meeting, Donna used **THERE** tools:

- **Think** through the meeting in advance. This includes considering the person's personality and communication style—how does she react to stress or confrontation? Analyzing personality traits and making notes will help you set the table for empathetic listening.
- **Hear** what the person has to say. Listen without interrupting.
- **Echo** back what you heard. Repeat as needed to get it correct. Ask questions to clarify as needed.
- **Relate** your own side of the story. Take care to share the facts. If you share feelings, make sure you use "I" statements that are specific to the incident.
- **Encourage** the person to repeat back what you said.

The goal of such listening is to hear and understand the person and the situation. This prevents misinformation and miscommunication when you are ready to problem-solve. Once both people fully understand both sides of the situation, they can begin resolving the conflict.

Applying STILL THERE to your own life

Think about a conflict in your own work life. How could you apply the **STILL THERE** method of listening?

The Situation: Write down your conflict situation. ______________________

____

____

STILL ...

Solo: Find a non-threatening and private way to set up meeting. For most people, it's easier to communicate in person. If that's not possible, telephones often work best, with a follow-through e-mail as needed.

- How and where will you set up the meeting?

Topic: State the topic in a non-judgmental way. Notice the difference between, "I want to understand why you are gone for so long at lunch." and "Why are you taking so much time off at lunch!"

- How will you state your topic?

Intention: Choose an intention that is honest and that implies collaboration and problem solving.

- What is your intention?

Length of the meeting: Give enough time to talk the issue through.

- How long will your meeting be?

Location and time: Choose a neutral and private place, where neither of you will be distracted.

- What are your location options? What are some of the least stressful times of day to have a meeting?

THERE ...

Think through the meeting in advance. Think about what you want to say. Make notes. Think about the person you're going to be talking to. What is his or her communication style? What are some of the personality traits you need to factor in? Consider the best way to approach the issue with each person.

- What are the main topics you want to cover? Do you have any hot buttons with this person? If so, what reminders do you need to calm yourself and stay an objective listener?

Hear what the person says. Your goal is to just listen to what the person has to say. Don't think about your own response.

- Notice the tone of voice, body language and word choice. Notice the emotional stance: Does the person seem angry, defensive, apologetic? Notice the person's phrasing: Does he or she say, "I think" or "I feel?"

Echo back what you heard.

- Try to mirror tone of voice and "thinking" or "feeling" phrases. Ask if you have heard correctly. Ask questions to clarify. Repeat as needed to get it correct.

Relate your own side of the story, referring to your notes as necessary.

- Take care to focus on the facts. Include the information he or she needs to fully understand your situation. Stick to the current conflict. If you share feelings, make sure you use "I" statements that are specific to the incident.

Encourage the person to repeat back what he or she heard you say.

- Listen carefully, making sure the person understands what you said and meant. Ask if you can add or clarify anything.

Set the table for empathetic listening

Developing your listening skills will help you soothe, understand and manage conflict. Listening is among the skills prized by today's companies. Here are some tips for creating a listening-friendly setting.

- Minimize noise and distractions. Turn off cell phones and background music and hold phone calls. If you expect any interruptions, let the other person know in advance.
- Be hospitable. When appropriate, offer something to drink and eat.
- Act calm and unhurried. If you need to have a time limit on the meeting, let the other person know in advance.
- Watch your language. Speak slowly and clearly. Don't use terms or acronyms your listener may not understand.
- Use phrases that invite communication and show you are there to listen: "I'd like you to share..." "I'm ready to listen..." "Take your time. There's no hurry." "I want to understand..." "I'm not sure I fully understood. I need to ask another question or two?"
- Honor your intuition. If you hear something that sounds false, strained or wrong, ask questions and gather more information. Try to understand what felt wrong to you.
- Turn off your own hot buttons. Try to remove yourself emotionally from the issue.
- Don't be afraid to take a break. When you feel tired or distracted, or you see the other person losing focus, take a short time-out: "I really want to concentrate on what you're saying. Let's take a short coffee break and return in five minutes."
- Protect yourself against the torrents. Empathetic listening is one thing and being trapped by a non-stop talker is another. Protect yourself from those torrential talkers by putting a time limit on the conversation with such people. Let them know you'll start with five minutes each. Continue with 10-15 minutes each, checking for understanding frequently. Gently interrupt if you need to, to keep on track and on time.

Test your own listening latitudes

"I'm a very good listener," Mary Ann insisted, when her boss invited her to a class on effective listening. She then spent ten minutes telling her boss what an amazing listener she was.

You've probably found yourself around a lot of self-proclaimed "great" listeners. Here's a way to notice your own listening skills. Keep a listening list for one day. Ask yourself:

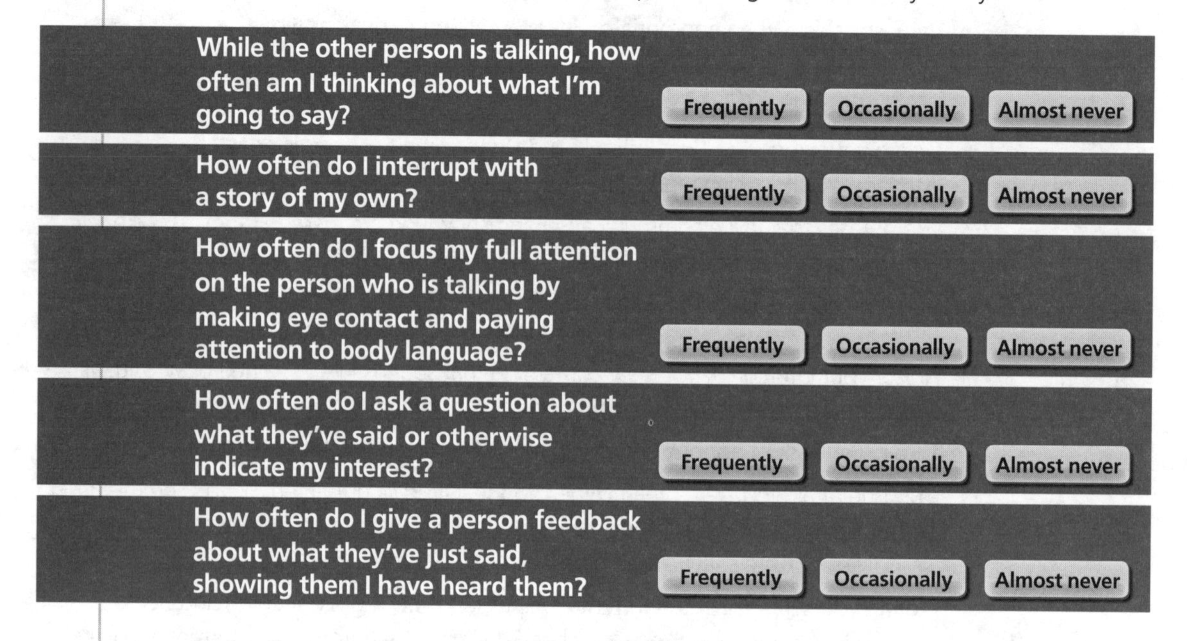

While the other person is talking, how often am I thinking about what I'm going to say?	Frequently	Occasionally	Almost never
How often do I interrupt with a story of my own?	Frequently	Occasionally	Almost never
How often do I focus my full attention on the person who is talking by making eye contact and paying attention to body language?	Frequently	Occasionally	Almost never
How often do I ask a question about what they've said or otherwise indicate my interest?	Frequently	Occasionally	Almost never
How often do I give a person feedback about what they've just said, showing them I have heard them?	Frequently	Occasionally	Almost never

Notice the areas where you can improve. You might ask a few trusted friends for help. You'll be surprised at how quickly your listening skills will deepen. The better listener you are, the fewer miscommunications you'll have. Miscommunication is at the core of many conflicts.

Tuning in on who's listening to you

Now, look at some of the questions on the test and analyze the listening skills of those you interact with on a daily basis. Is your boss a good listener? Your colleagues? Your direct reports? Your vendors? If not, as part of your conflict defusing techniques, you might want to model good listening skills and also start asking them to repeat for understanding:

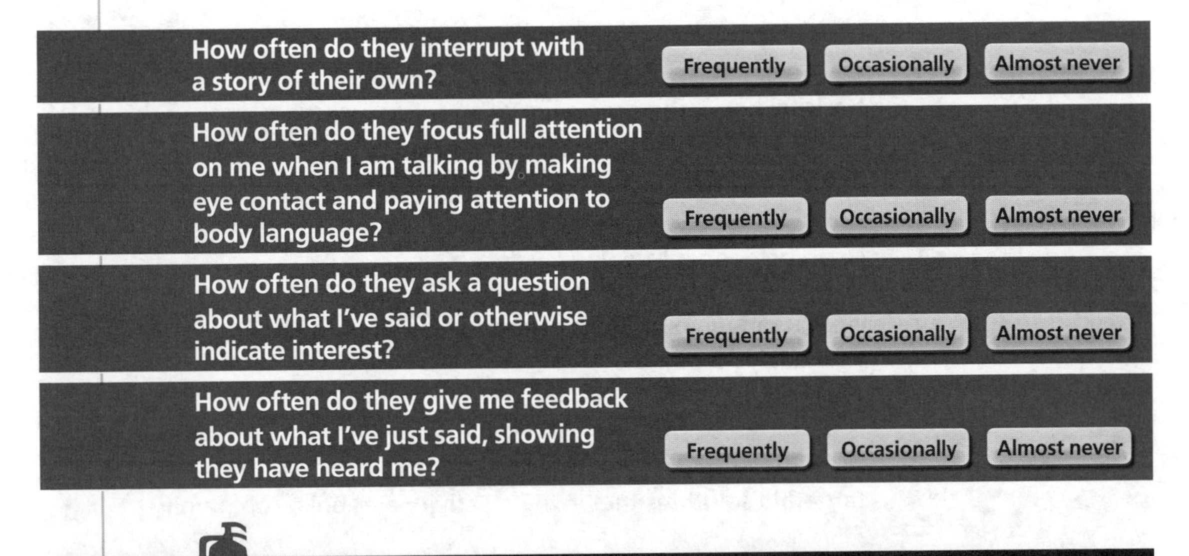

How often do they interrupt with a story of their own?	Frequently	Occasionally	Almost never
How often do they focus full attention on me when I am talking by making eye contact and paying attention to body language?	Frequently	Occasionally	Almost never
How often do they ask a question about what I've said or otherwise indicate interest?	Frequently	Occasionally	Almost never
How often do they give me feedback about what I've just said, showing they have heard me?	Frequently	Occasionally	Almost never

Conflict Quenchers

Hearing aids

Before you go into an intense listening situation, calm yourself by listening to a favorite piece of music. Or read aloud a favorite poem or call a friend for a quick affirming conversation.

Notice the sounds of silence

Take a one-minute silence break and notice the sounds around you. If you can, sit still and close your eyes. Take some deep breaths. Notice your inner voices. If they are agitated, say something affirming, such as "I will easily be able to listen and hear what I need to hear."

In this chapter . . .

You've learned how to successfully listen to a conflict situation by:

- **C** — **Concentrating on the facts, rather than the emotions**
- **O** — Opening yourself to opportunity for growth and learning
- **N** — **Noticing how others view life**
- **F** — Forming new ways of looking at a situation
- **L** — **Learning deeper listening levels**
- **I** — **Incorporating your priorities and values along with your analytical skills**
- **C** — Connecting through problem solving
- **T** — **Targeting solutions that invite creativity and build community**

CONFLICT EXTINGUISHER

From Clash to Conversation: Forging Positive Solutions

Georgia was comfortable that her listening session with Donna had gone well. She felt she understood the situation and was ready to problem solve. But she had a pressing meeting in 10 minutes, so she said, "I want to come up with a solution as soon as possible. Why don't you talk things over with your husband and mother-in-law and meet me tomorrow morning at 9:00."

Donna nodded.

As Georgia prepared for her next meeting, she thought about her sister, hundreds of miles away, who was caring for their mother in her home. She felt guilty that she hadn't even called this week.

Later that afternoon, Georgia's boss Evelyn called, saying she had received a complaint about preferential treatment regarding lunch breaks. Georgia felt a rush of fear and anger. She had worked so hard to make sure all her employees liked and trusted her. Why hadn't the employee come and talked to her? Who was so disloyal and so unhappy they would go directly to her boss?

"I'm surprised you haven't handled this more proactively, Georgia," Evelyn said. "I understand it's been going on for weeks."

"Donna is one of my best workers. I wasn't sure this was really a problem until last week and I wanted to give her a chance to ..."

"I don't need details. When will you fix this?"

"Donna and I are meeting again tomorrow."

"Good. I'd like to hear from you after the meeting."

Georgia was shaking when she hung up the phone. Evelyn was always so abrupt and so quick to judge. She knew she should have met with Donna sooner, but she'd been swamped. Georgia could feel a headache marching across her forehead. Now the pressure was building. Who else on the team was going behind her back, and was her own job in danger?

Fraught in the middle

Think of a time when you were in Georgia's situation, with conflict from two directions. One person demanded you act one way and the other person expected you to act another way. For extra insight, share the story of your conflict with a friend or co-worker.

- What were the conflicts?
- How did you feel?
- Given your personality, what were your challenges?
- What actions did you take?
- What help did you seek?
- How did you resolve the conflict?
- Were you satisfied? What would have made the process better?

Conflicts from all directions

As the day progressed, Georgia felt more and more stressed. She kept wondering who complained and where she had gone wrong. Her confidence was near zero when she called her friend Carolyn, who had a managerial position in community relations. Carolyn agreed to meet her for a quick coffee and a consult.

The moment Georgia saw Carolyn, she felt more relaxed. Carolyn was not afraid of conflict and of direct, honest communication. She could help Georgia put things in perspective.

Carolyn admitted she too found Evelyn's style difficult and abrasive. "But for now," she advised, "give the conflict a ***REST****."*

Carolyn explained what she meant. She suggested a simple four-step method that would help Georgia give her fears and emotions a "rest" so she could concentrate on the "rest" of the problem.

Here is the **REST** approach:

- **Review** the facts. Separate facts from gossip, hearsay or opinions.
- **Eliminate** the emotions. Georgia needed to find a safe way to identify and express her emotions, then separate those feelings from the problem.
- **See both sides** of the story. Georgia needed to look at the situation from Donna's point of view and to imagine how she might respond.
- **Think** about commonality. Georgia could list the things she and Donna had in common and explore mutually beneficial solutions.

The problem seemed smaller and more manageable when she gave it the **REST** treatment.

Review the facts—*Donna was staying a half hour later than authorized at lunch at least two days a week. Georgia's job was to keep the department running smoothly and productively.*

Eliminate the emotions. *After talking to Carolyn, Georgia was calm and unemotional once more.*

See both sides. *Georgia needed to treat everyone equally and fairly and have her department comply with company rules and productivity standards. Donna needed to feel like she could take care of her mother-in-law and still do her job.*

Think about what they had in common. *Georgia felt they both wanted to do their work right. They both wanted to feel they were responsible women, at work and at home. They both wanted to feel respected and appreciated. Georgia kept these mutual needs in mind as she thought about solutions.*

Preparing for problem solving—REST assured

The more prepared you are, the more comfortable and flexible you'll be during the conversation.

Think of a conflict you are facing now. It can be challenging to separate facts from feelings and to work through the emotions the conflict brings up. To practice broadening your thinking, do this exercise with a friend, colleague or even a family member. Give it the **REST** test:

Review the facts. Separate facts from gossip, hearsay or opinions. See if you can define the essence of the conflict in one sentence.

- The facts: ____________________

Eliminate the emotions. Figure out what you are feeling. Then express those feelings through journaling, conversation with a friend or saying them out loud to yourself.

- Your feelings: ____________________

See both sides of the story. Think about how you would want to be treated if you were in the other person's situation.

- Your side: ____________________
- The other side: ____________________

Think about what you have in common and explore mutually beneficial solutions. Try to imagine what the other person will say and want.

- What you have in common: ____________________
- What the other party might say and want: ____________________
- Some possible solutions: ____________________

The cactus conversation: Doing your best in a prickly situation

Donna's shoulders were hunched as she trudged into the conference room. She barely looked at Georgia.

"I know we both want an easy solution to this problem," Georgia said, pushing away the glowering image of Evelyn that suddenly came into her head. "I know you're going through a lot and I really admire the way you're caring for your mother-in-law. What suggestions do you have?"

"I hoped my husband would be helping me out more, but he says he can't," Donna said. Georgia heard the anger and bitterness in her voice and wondered about the conflicts Donna was dealing with at home.

Georgia took a deep breath and sat still. She thought of what she and Donna had in common—their desire to do a good job, be responsible and be appreciated for what they accomplished. She thought of her own mother and wished she could just let Donna have the time off she needed.

"If only my husband could help more, I wouldn't be going through this," Donna said, her voice rising. "I told him I might lose my job."

"Donna, I know this is upsetting to you. Let's think about other options. What about home health; have you looked into that? Any neighbor who'd be willing to help out a day or two a week? What about trying her in day care a day or two a week—just as an experiment?"

Donna nodded wearily. "I'm just so tired. I didn't want to get into another argument with my husband over this. He says this is family business and we should take care of it ourselves. But I'm the one who's taking care of it."

"It sounds like you're doing an admirable job," Georgia said. "But you need to take care of yourself and your job, as well. What are your options?"

"I'll talk to my neighbor's daughter—she's back home, dropped out of college. She might help out for a while."

"So you'll start with your neighbor's daughter to help you out?" Georgia said. "You might want to talk to Human Resources as well—they can be a great resource on elder care."

"I'll do that," Donna said. "It will be a relief to talk about this."

"So, tomorrow can I count on you taking a one-hour lunch?"

Donna nodded. She shook her head. "I bet everyone is mad at me for taking off that extra time. I'll let them know what's going on."

Coming to terms: Un-stickering the cactus

Everyone has his or her own style of dealing with conflict. Some people are swift and decisive; others more gentle and pondering. Georgia tended to be a people pleaser. If you were coaching Georgia and giving her feedback, how would you answer these questions? If possible, talk these over with a group:

- In this situation, how could this people-pleasing tendency get in her way?
- How could this tendency benefit her and the department?
- What tools did Georgia use in her problem solving? (For example: How did she use listening skills?)
- What did she do when she felt uncertain?
- What did she do when she felt her emotions getting in the way?
- What would have improved the way she handled the conversation?

One of the best ways to hone your own conflict-solving skills is to learn from other people. How would you have handled the situation with Donna?

The REST of the story: Meeting with Evelyn and the staff

Georgia was nervous about her meeting with Evelyn. Even though she'd solved the problem, Evelyn's dismissive manner could make Georgia feel like she was incompetent. She decided to try the ***REST*** *approach with Evelyn:*

- **Review** the facts. *Someone from Georgia's department had complained to Evelyn about Georgia's management abilities.*
- **Eliminate** the emotions. *This was hard for Georgia. Every time she thought of someone going behind her back to Evelyn, she felt a rush of anger and fear. The fact was, someone in her department felt uncomfortable and upset. She could be grateful Evelyn had communicated with her so quickly and directly.*
- **See both sides** of the story. *From Evelyn's point of view, dissension in departments lowered productivity and made her look bad. Georgia knew that Evelyn wanted to be respected and acknowledged for being on top of things.*
- **Think** about commonality. *Georgia and Evelyn both wanted the company to do well. They both wanted to do their jobs well.*

Evelyn was on the phone when Georgia entered her office. She motioned for Georgia to sit down. As usual, she did not smile, but Georgia reminded herself, this was not personal; this was just Evelyn.

"Well?" Evelyn said, as she hung up the phone.

"My meeting with Donna went well. We discussed options and tomorrow she'll be taking a one-hour lunch, as usual."

"Good."

Evelyn glanced at her calendar and Georgia said, "I want to thank you for telling me about the employee who complained to you. I appreciate how quickly and directly you communicated that to me. I'm going to meet with the staff and explain the situation."

"Excellent," Evelyn said. Her voice had lost its impatient tone and she was looking right at Georgia. "I'm glad you were willing to pay attention to the situation. Not everyone is willing to address a conflict."

Georgia smiled. She was eager to use REST as a model for talking to her staff, explaining the situation, letting them know that each of them was important to her and that she was always willing to help work through personal issues that conflicted with work schedules.

What went right and what could have been better?

Georgia and her friend Carolyn had a debriefing meeting the next week. Carolyn suggested Georgia use the conflict as a learning tool.

These are some of the questions that Georgia used in analyzing the situation:

- What was Georgia's role in the conflict?
- What could she have done to catch the problem earlier?
- How could she have improved her solutions style?
- What is the best thing that could happen from this conflict?
- How could she use the conflict situation to better the workplace?

Think of one of your recent conflicts and ask yourself these questions:

- What was your role in the conflict?
- What could you have done to catch or notice the problem earlier?
- How could you have improved your solutions style?
- What is the best thing that happened from this conflict?

Remember, conflict often inspires meaningful and necessary change. Here are some tips for creating a solutions-oriented atmosphere for problem-solving.

- Think about collaboration and coming to an agreement rather than winning or getting your way.
- Be open to compromise but don't give in just to avoid or stop a conflict.
- Keep asking questions until you feel you understand the other person's position.

Conflict Quenchers

Move toward compatible solutions

- Talk through your strategy with a friend or write it out.
- Talk to yourself on walks or drives.
- Let it go and look for another way if you can't get your way.
- Be sincere when you're offering solutions.
- Speak directly without being didactic or pushy.

Stretch time

Take time out when you're feeling uncertain. Use phrases such as:

- "Let me take a minute to think that over."
- "You've brought up some interesting points."
- "I need a few minutes to digest the information."

When you feel yourself tightening up physically and emotionally, ask yourself, "What do I fear?"

Go wild

When searching for solutions, have fun brainstorming wild solutions. Perhaps you all go on a cruise and forget all about your problems. Perhaps you take turns—one day you have your way and the next the other person does things her way. Perhaps you divide the department in half—one-half does it her way and the other your way. Then you switch sides for a week. The wilder and wilder you think, the more chances you have of coming up with a creative solution that works for everyone.

In this chapter ...

You've learned how to solve a conflict situation by:

C **Concentrating on the facts, rather than the emotions**

O Opening yourself to opportunity for growth and learning

N Noticing how others view life

F Forming new ways of looking at a situation

L **Learning deeper listening levels**

I Incorporating your priorities and values along with your analytical skills

C **Connecting through problem solving**

T **Targeting solutions that invite creativity and build community**

CONFLICT EXTINGUISHER

Chapter Seven

Into the Fray: Taking Care of Yourself in Difficult and Emotionally Charged Situations

Flattening the emotional fizz: Separating fact from feeling

*If you looked into Sandra's car, you would think she was having a very lively argument with an expert debater. But Sandra was involved in a lively monologue with her internal debater and a host of **WISs** (**W**ish **I**'d **S**aids).*

*Perhaps you've had an experience similar to this one: After lunch, a co-worker rushed up to Sandra, her mouth tense, her fists clenched. Suddenly, she was yelling about a report Sandra did last week. Something was wrong with it, she shouted, and Sandra knew everyone in the office could hear her. Sandra was caught totally off guard. Before she could think of a way to stop the angry words or move her co-worker into a more private area, the woman was gone. Sandra left with a crowd of **WISs**.*

*The moment she was alone in her office, the **WISs** danced in. Brilliant, calm, insightful remarks, cunning facts, cooling questions that would have stopped the tirade.*

*The **WISs** trailed Sandra the rest of the day. They chattered wisely in the restroom, coached her while she drank a soda and followed her out to the car, where they vied for her attention all the way home.*

Learning more about dealing with uncomfortable situations and difficult or angry people will help you turn those **WISs** into **TISs** (**T**hen **I** **S**aids) or **WOWs** (**W**ords **o**f **W**isdom).

Slow them down

If you are the victim of a surprise verbal attack or if a person becomes angry when you're problem solving together, try to defuse and soften the energy by taking some of these actions:

- Speak softly and slowly.
- Acknowledge their feelings. "I hear that you're upset ..."
- Instead of defending yourself and possibly escalating the anger, ask clarifying questions. Show your desire to understand the problem and their point of view.
- Show them you are listening carefully by throwing in validating phrases such as, "I hear what you are saying." "Does that mean you think that..." "That's interesting. Tell me more."

- Notice if they are using thinking, feeling, seeing or hearing words in their arguments and mirror back that language.
- Use "I" statements when you state your point of view. Focus on the pertinent facts, your feelings and what you need.
- Bring the conversation back to center if you get off track.
- If staying on track is not working, steer the conversation onto a related but less volatile subject. See if you can regain common ground before moving back into the problem.
- If the anger seems to be escalating, help yourself stay centered by taking all the emotion out of your voice and speaking in a flat, automatic tone. That puts your focus on content, rather than on any feelings of discomfort or intimidation.
- If the person becomes verbally abusive, say, "I can't let you talk to me this way. I'll be happy to talk to you about this when you are calm." Then leave the room or gently hang up the phone.

Icing down anger

Erica could feel the hostility when she entered the room. She had asked her manager for this meeting because she could no longer stand working with Ashley. They were supposed to be planning the spring health fair together, but so far, Erica had done all the work. Every time they made a list of who was going to do what, Erica did her share and Ashley did nothing.

When Erica tried to talk to Ashley about her part of the project, Ashley narrowed her eyes and said, "You are such a control freak. I have planned hundreds of events. I work on my own timetable, not yours." Since that conversation, Ashley had been giving Erica the silent treatment. When Erica walked into the break room, Ashley would glare at her, then abruptly leave. Erica felt people were talking behind her back. Ashley's anger, silent though it was, was getting to Erica.

As the days went by, Erica worried that Ashley's "timetable" would be too late. When Erica told Ashley she was going to ask their boss for help in solving their conflict, Ashley looked daggers at Erica and said in a menacing voice, "You have no idea what you're getting yourself into." All week, Erica had felt Ashley's anger directed at her and wondered what she was getting into. Now, she wondered if she could keep her cool and not wither under Ashley's disdain.

CHILL before the meeting

People who are angry can be intimidating and rob you of your confidence. Plus, their random and seemingly unfair behavior can ignite your own emotions. To keep from being consumed in the conflagration, here are a few **CHILL** tips to help you prepare for such a meeting. Whether this is a meeting with a manager or other facilitator, an informal conversation between you and the other person, or even a spontaneous confrontation, **CHILL** helps you get prepared, focused and centered.

- **Create notes** that cover the important points. Just the act of writing down notes helps you remember the focus and your common goals, even when you're confronted by someone who is upset or angry.
- **Help** yourself stay centered, reminding yourself, this is not personal.
- **Invite** the contentious person to speak first.
- **Let** the contentious person be the first to offer solutions.
- **Leave** emotions out of it and keep yourself focused on your common goals.

Though Erica was not leading this meeting, she used the CHILL technique to prepare herself. She knew that she sometimes stumbled verbally when someone got aggressive with her. She made notes, stating the facts. She included their shared timetable, with responsibilities they had both agreed to complete.

Erica decided that every time she felt tense and uncomfortable, she would simply take a deep breath. She would remind herself, this is not personal.

When the boss asked what the problem was, Erica would invite Ashley to tell her side of the story first. Erica didn't even know Ashley's side of the story, since Ashley hadn't spoken to her in days. She figured listening could help prepare her for whatever misery Ashley hoped to heap upon her. She would also try to get Ashley to offer solutions. "Our goal is to make sure the health fair is a success," Erica reminded herself.

The CHILL technique worked well for Erica. She let Ashley speak first. Ashley told a disjointed, emotional story about how bossy and anal Erica was. "I'm an adult," Ashley said, in what Erica thought was a very childish way. "I don't need HER telling ME how to do MY job."

Erica clamped her mouth shut so she wouldn't interrupt with a righteous defense. She consulted her notes when she told her story and stuck to the facts. She spoke slowly and clearly, trying to keep any anger out of her voice.

Ashley did have a solution, which she delivered in a sarcastic way. Erica was disappointed the boss didn't comment on Ashley's attitude. Instead, he just listened, nodding his head occasionally. Ashley suggested they divide up the project. Each would work independently and report to a third person.

Erica felt a sense of relief at her boss's agreement to that solution, even though her personal issues with Ashley were not solved. She still did not understand why Ashley thought she was so controlling and why Ashley hadn't done her share of the work.

Erica stewed over the meeting all evening, then decided, "Ashley is not my business."

She decided to either avoid Ashley or look for genuine ways she could praise her work, if she ever did any work. Erica also decided to talk through the situation with a friend, so she could get the anger out of her system.

CHILL without supervision

Most of us have been in situations where the supervisor is part of the problem. If Erica were on her own with Ashley, how might she have approached the problem? Answer these questions, as if you were advising Erica:

- What does Erica need before she talks to Ashley? (For example, does she need more facts about Ashley's work? Does she need more information about Ashley or the impact of being late for the project?)
- How should she prepare for a conversation with Ashley? Using the CHILL method, what factors does she need to take into account?
- What could go wrong during the conversation?
- What sort of support or backup plan would you recommend?

Being a back-seat driver: The cool art of observation

A lot happened during the planning session and Nan did none of it. She did not get involved in the heated argument about the venue for the annual meeting. She did not contribute to the cutting conversation about the person who handled the last annual meeting. She did not correct Jordan when he said that her team was late in getting the budget prepared. Someone else did that for her. She offered suggestions for speakers, but didn't break in when someone else suggested a speaker they had never heard who was much more expensive. A lot happened during the planning session and Nan was the only member of the committee who was truly watching and listening.

"Two years ago, I would have been right in there, making my voice heard, correcting people, sticking up for myself," she told a co-worker later that afternoon. "But I have seen that doesn't work around here. The more you correct, the more someone defends. For me, it's valuable to truly listen to and observe the interactions, then see where I can make the most impact."

There are times when listening is the most powerful conflict management tool you have. There are other times when speaking out in the group is your one legitimate chance to be heard. Hone your own balance of these skills. Make your words count when you speak and make your silence matter, as you observe and learn.

Taking the wheel or being on a ride: A balancing act

Think of a recent meeting:

- Are there times you wished you had spoken out?
- If so, what was the situation?
- What prevented you from speaking?
- What could you have done differently?
- Are there times you wished you hadn't said anything?
- If so, what was the situation?
- What prevented you from sitting silently?
- What could you have done differently?

Remember, you have the power to use your skills, both verbal and listening, to your best advantage, in every situation.

Throw like a girl … problem solve like a woman

When is something a personality difference and when is there a gender issue involved? Here are some situations that could have gender implications.

Supervising the young and relentless

Carolyn had to confront one of her team members about turning in shoddy work. Frank was new to the team and fairly young. Carolyn wanted to give him the benefit of the doubt, so she scheduled a meeting, using ***STILL THERE*** *techniques. She felt confident in her listening and problem solving skills, although she knew Frank had an attitude—he was right, and everyone else was wrong. She'd heard him making disparaging remarks about women co-workers. Carolyn had prepared for the meeting, including creating a written report for Frank that would show him the specs for the work.*

When she asked Frank to tell her why the quality of his work was down, he said, "It's good enough." He crossed his arms and leaned back in his chair and stared at the ceiling.

Carolyn felt like calling off the meeting, but she kept going, stating the facts and what she needed from him. She asked him to repeat back what she had said and Frank answered, "The work I'm doing is just fine."

He then took the report she had handed him, tossed it onto the table and left the room.

Carolyn felt like ordering him back into the room for an apology. But instead she took a few moments to analyze the situation. She wondered if such a "macho" man resented taking instruction from a woman.

She wrote up a memo of the meeting. Then she let it sit for an hour and reread it, making sure it was factual and not tinged with her emotions. Then she wrote an e-mail to Frank, letting him know she expected his work to conform to company standards. She reread the e-mail before sending it, making sure it was clear and concise. Carolyn knew she now had to document everything and not waver, no matter how unpleasantly Frank behaved.

From good girl to strong woman

Linda had a competent and efficient supervisor who was pretty easy to work with. But one thing he said drove Linda up the wall. When he wanted her to do something extra, he dropped by her office and said, "Be a good girl and ..."

Linda was 40 years old and way beyond wanting to be a "good girl." She didn't mind being an extraordinary employee or a loyal worker or even "a good sport," as he referred to the men when he asked them to do something extra.

Linda tried to tell herself, "It's only a word," but the word seemed like a put-down to her.

She tried to imagine how her boss would react if she talked to him about the issue. She thought he would be open to her comments. She figured he wasn't aware of his language. She calculated the worst that could happen: He could blow up and she could lose her job. But this "good girl" business was so stressful that she felt it could be worth it.

Linda waited for the incident to occur again. When he came into her office and "good girled" her, she asked if he had five minutes for a brief conversation. He said he did. Linda got right to the point. "You are a great boss and I enjoy working for you. But I need to tell you one thing that is bothering me. Do you have time to listen?"

He looked worried but nodded yes.

"When you come into my office and ask me to 'Be a good girl' and do something for you, I feel demeaned. Do you ask the men to be 'good boys'? I am happy to do extra tasks but I need you to change your language. I'd like you to ask me simply if I have time to do this extra task. "

Her boss looked stunned. She couldn't tell if he was fuming or thinking. She let the silence be there.

Finally he said, "I had no idea I was offending you. I wish you had spoken up sooner. I saw the words as a term of affection, but I can certainly use other language."

Linda sat still after he left. She couldn't tell if he felt angry or resentful. But two days later he dropped by with a smile and asked, "Do you have time to do this extra task for me?"

Linda was lucky—she had a boss who was unaware of his behavior and was willing to change. Another type of boss could have ignored her request or been too intimidating to confront.

What would Linda's options be if she did not have a supportive boss? What advice would you have for her?

Sorting through gender issues

There are plenty of great men in the workplace. There also are men who are consciously or subconsciously programmed to ignore, dismiss, underestimate, interrupt or put down women. When you come across these men:

- Separate problems from personalities.
- Understand your own gender-activated trigger points.
- Analyze the man's intentions and motives. Try to find out or understand why he is acting this way.
- If the situation allows, bring the problem to the man's attention, stating the facts, your feelings and what you want. The man may not be aware of his behavior.
- Seek help when your own proven techniques don't work. Consult with other women to learn from their experience and get their advice. Consult with trusted men friends or colleagues, seeking to find out if you're misinterpreting any communications or behavior. If you have an empathetic supervisor, consult him or her.

Hurdling the hierarchies

The non-listening employee, the know-everything co-worker, the resentful report, the impossible boss …

Most of us could list many more less-than-ideal personalities we have had to work with, work for or supervise. What about a difficult personality you are currently dealing with? Think of ways you might reduce your conflict potential by using the CHILL technique with a difficult person:

- Where is he or she in the hierarchy of command?
- What type of personality does he or she have?
- What kinds of conflicts come up between you?
- How have you been handling the issues?
- What steps could you take to do things more effectively?

Setting the ground rules for group conflict conversations

Before you go into a conflict-solving conversation with people who might be or become angry, contentious or aggressive, agree on conversational guidelines. (These guidelines also work for small informal conflict situations, when there are just two of you.) Here are some suggestions to incorporate:

- Each person gets to speak for a set period of time without interruptions.
- There is no shouting, name calling or personal insults.
- The group agrees to consider all ideas for potential solutions.
- The group agrees to take time outs when emotions or anger threaten to get in the way.
- The group agrees to ask for help from an outside party if they get stuck.

Setting the stage

Select a neutral meeting place, where all parties can be free from interruption. Try to make the room as comfortable as possible, via lighting and temperature. Think about your seating configuration. Make sure all participants can easily see and hear one another.

Consider the message you are making with the seating configuration. If the meeting has an acknowledged leader or facilitator, a rectangular table can be appropriate. If you want more of an atmosphere of equality, consider sitting in a circle. For a more open feeling, have a simple circle of chairs, with no table to hide behind.

If you anticipate a long meeting, plan a break and include food and drink. Just the act of eating together gives you something in common. When possible, avoid foods such as sugar that fuel nervousness and hyperactivity.

Some groups pass around an object to indicate who has the right to speak. If you want to try such an object, choose a symbol appropriate for your organization. You may choose a cup with your company's logo. A bowl or some kind of circular object could also work.

If anyone gets verbally abusive, stop the meeting. Remind everyone of the agreed upon rules. Ask if everyone still agrees to those rules. If not, you may need to continue the problem solving later, with a mediator. If you're worried about someone getting verbally abusive or out of hand, consider meeting in a public place, such as a coffee shop.

Simmer down a sizzling situation

It's important to know your people when you're trying to facilitate a conflict resolution. These ideas may work with some people and may not appeal to others:

- Have everyone write down everything they dislike about the conflict and everything they like about the people involved. You can do this before the meeting or as an anger-quencher during the meeting.
- When you know your group, you can try humor to cool things down. If you're using humor, make the joke on you and do it without undermining your credibility. The humor can be a reminder that you're all human.

Conflict Quenchers

Be a sport: Take a time out

All the best athletes and teams do this. Don't worry when you don't know what to say or do. Sometimes you just need to take a break so you can gain perspective and recover your cool and confidence.

Let off steam by having fun

Do something that relaxes you and takes your mind away from conflict. Take a walk, do a crossword puzzle, read a mystery, have an evening with friends. Renewing yourself helps put difficult people in perspective.

In this chapter ...

You've learned how to solve a conflict situation by:

- **C**: **Concentrating on the facts, rather than the emotions**
- **O**: **Opening yourself to opportunity for growth and learning**
- **N**: Noticing how others view life
- **F**: **Forming new ways of looking at a situation**
- **L**: Learning deeper listening levels
- **I**: Incorporating your priorities and values along with your analytical skills
- **C**: **Connecting through problem solving**
- **T**: **Targeting solutions that invite creativity and build community**

Chapter Eight

"Feeling" Your Way: Managing Your Emotions

They show up unannounced and suddenly have huge opinions about something that is really none of their business. Instead of sitting quietly through a meeting, they whisper and vie for your attention. When you are trying to concentrate, they barge right in and rant on about a situation you'd really rather not discuss. How can you manage such a mouthy and unwieldy group—how can you manage your emotions?

Faster than a speeding bullet, more powerful than a locomotive, our super-charged emotions can easily rise up to save our day or to sink our ship. Noticing, understanding and appropriately communicating these emotions can improve the way we manage conflict.

Keep CALM

The **CALM** approach is one way to take stirred-up emotions and move them into meaningful communication.

Here are the steps:

- **Create** a list of the issues and events that are bothering you.
- **Acknowledge** the facts and acknowledge your feelings.
- **Leave time** for your stress-soothers.
- **Manage** to express yourself appropriately.

Create a list

Erica felt much better since her meeting with her boss and Ashley regarding working on the health fair. Erica was relieved to be responsible for her own work and not for Ashley's.

Yet even though the main problem was solved, the emotional underbelly was still there. The moment Erica walked into work, she felt the tension eating away at her. When Erica walked into the break room, Ashley would often whisper to the person sitting next to her and then laugh. One day Erica said hello to Ashley, and Ashley turned away and said nothing. Erica felt mortified and furious.

"Ignore Ashley," a friend advised.

"She probably doesn't trust you," another said.

"Find out what's bugging her," another friend said.

Erica remembered being treated the same way by a girl in high school. Erica had vowed that no one would treat her that way again. Yet here she was in the same situation. Erica decided to make a list of the things that were stressing her. The list included:

- Ashley not speaking to me
- Ashley possibly talking about me to other people
- Ashley treating me like I am dirt
- A feeling that other people think I am untrustworthy because I went to the boss with a problem about a co-worker
- A feeling that people are talking about me
- A feeling that this is all very unfair

Acknowledge the facts and acknowledge your feelings

Just writing the list made Erica feel more grounded. She read her list aloud several times and was surprised to see she had only a few facts and lots of feelings and conjecture.

"Ashley not speaking to me" was not accurate, when she really thought about it. Ashley had spoken to her at meetings—not warmly, but civilly. The only real fact was, "Ashley did not speak to me when I said hello in the break room."

Leave time for your stress-soothers

Still, the more she thought about Ashley ignoring her and possibly spreading nasty rumors about her, the angrier Erica felt. She began biting her fingernails, something she had not done since high school. At home, she snapped at her husband for no good reason. She was constantly on the verge of tears. Erica's silent rage knotted itself into her stomach, and she could barely eat without getting a stomachache.

"Maybe you need to relax a little," her husband said one night after she had stormed away from the dinner table because he had asked if there were more potatoes.

Reaching for a tissue, Erica realized he was right.

That night, she made another list—things that sounded stress-free and relaxing. Reading, walking, listening to music, talking to friends, going to the movies with her husband. Erica realized she had ignored all her usual coping skills. She asked her husband out for a date that Friday evening. She called a girlfriend and scheduled lunch. She was too wrought up to concentrate on a book, but she picked up a cooking magazine and looked over the recipes.

She also remembered she could take a deep breath when she needed to calm down. She could stand, stretch or take a five-minute walk and reconnect with herself.

The more she practiced her stress soothers, the more Erica noticed when tension began to grip her. When she started to bite her fingernails, she took a breath and smiled. She said to herself, "I am going to like everyone. I am going to be positive." Even though she didn't quite believe that, it helped calm her.

Manage to express yourself appropriately

At lunch, Erica talked to her girlfriend about the Ashley issue.

"Why don't you think of something good about her?" her girlfriend suggested. "Maybe she thinks you don't like her."

Erica considered her friend's advice. Maybe Ashley felt paranoid about Erica. Erica decided she was going to take action. She decided to:

- Analyze her own behavior and try to imagine what that behavior might have looked like to Ashley.
- Explore how her earlier experience in high school might have affected her reactions to Ashley.
- Find something good about Ashley and praise her.
- Figure out an appropriate way to explain how she felt when Ashley did not speak to her in the break room.

Erica found something praiseworthy two days later—a poster announcing the health fair. Ashley had done a remarkable job of designing it and Erica knew she could sincerely praise her. She walked into Ashley's office and said, "Do you have a minute?"

Ashley looked up and gave her a "whatever" look.

"I just saw the poster you designed. It's stunning," Erica said. "That poster is going to get a lot of people interested in checking out the health fair."

Ashley stared at her for a moment. "I like design work," she said.

"I can see why. You have a gift for it."

"Thanks," Ashley said. "I never thought I'd hear a compliment from you, of all people."

That remark startled Erica. When she asked why, Ashley told her she thought Erica had been talking behind her back. She didn't trust Erica and she didn't trust herself not to scream at her, so she just didn't speak, when possible.

Erica took a deep breath, sat down and said, "When I said hello to you in the break room and you didn't answer, I felt so hurt, left out and angry. I just really needed to tell you that."

"I didn't even hear you say hello," Ashley told her. "I just thought you were ignoring me."

They looked at each other and laughed. Like many emotional conflicts, this one was silently fueled by miscommunication. Thanks to the ***CALM*** *approach, Erica was able to turn her anger and hurt into understanding.*

Keeping CALM in times of anger

What are some of the unfair and unjust issues that are angering you right now? Think about a situation that causes you emotional volatility. Now look at that issue with **CALM** …

- Create a list of the issues that are bothering you. Don't censor yourself; list everything that comes to mind.
- Acknowledge the facts and acknowledge your feelings. Read through your list aloud. Star the facts. Circle the feelings. Sometimes just noticing the difference is calming.

You may feel angry, left out, shamed or hurt. Let yourself feel those uncomfortable feelings and try to understand where they come from.

- Leave time for your stress-soothers. Write down things that relax you and help you feel calm and centered. Pick two things from your list to do right away. Make a list of small things you can do to de-stress at work.
- Manage to express yourself appropriately. Just calming down and reviewing the facts and the feelings may give you insights. Ask yourself:
  — What is triggering your feelings?
  — How can you gain a deeper understanding of the situation?
  — Can you let go of any feelings?
  — Which feelings do you need to express?
  — Is it appropriate to express yourself to the person triggering the feelings?
  — Is it better to express your feelings to a safe third person?
  — What else do you need to do to manage your feelings?
  — How can you forgive the other person or forgive yourself?

Give it a REST

Before you rush out to express your righteous anger, take a few moments to write down what you want to say. If you can, put the piece of paper away for a couple of hours. Look at it again later and see if you still feel the same way. Better yet, sleep on it. You may discover a way to more diplomatically express yourself. You may discover you don't need to express yourself.

When you have angry or emotional feelings you want to express, try to talk in person. Avoid putting emotional information in an e-mail—it's too easy to misinterpret.

- Review the facts.
- Eliminate the emotions.
- See both sides of the story.
- Think about commonality.

Letting go without letting loose: The safety vent

Laura was furious at her manager—he had taken one of her best sales accounts and just given it to a new salesman. Laura did not want to confront or talk to him right now. He was too volatile, and she knew he would put the blame back on her. But she needed to do something with her anger. She called a friend and asked if she was up for a 20-minute "complaining" session.

When they got together, Laura set a timer and told her friend the whole rotten story of her boss. Laura was dramatic and emotional. She told her side of the story and she told it with all her anger and sense of outrage. At the end of 20 minutes, she stopped, thanked her friend and offered to do the same for her some time.

Laura felt much better. By speaking her outrage, she reduced her anger. She also thought of several other components of the story that she had not previously considered, components that would help her when she did confront her boss. She decided to document what had happened, citing all the facts and leaving out all the drama, for future reference.

Many of us have been in Laura's situation: We needed to express our anger, but we also needed to preserve our cool at work.

Think of a time when you really needed to vent but couldn't because of your employment circumstances:

- What was your situation?
- What prevented you from speaking out?
- What did you do?
- Who did you reach out to?
- How did you express your feelings?
- How did you feel afterwards?
- Was the venting helpful to you? What were the long-term results?
- What would you do differently if you had to face this situation again?

Keeping yourself cool: Managing emotions in meetings

Maria felt herself heating up during the meeting. Carl was criticizing her again. The last time she spoke up, she was criticized for being overly aggressive. Now she didn't know what to do. She was seething, but figured if she spoke she would make it worse.

"Maria, what do you think about the issues Carl was addressing?" the facilitator said.

"That's a good question," Maria said to the facilitator. "Let me think about that for a moment."

She knew she had to calm down. Some people were already scared by how assertive she was. She tried to put herself in their shoes. She remembered what her friend had told her: "Don't challenge people. Don't get in their faces. Don't try to prove you are better than they are."

Maria thought Carl was an arrogant, worthless, egoistic twit who should not be the head of a department. Maria thought if she said what she was actually thinking, she could be without a job.

She remembered her anger mantra, "It's not personal." Carl didn't even know her very well. He was criticizing her because of his own insecurity or anger.

Maria looked directly at the facilitator. She spoke clearly and slowly. "I have a different take on the situation," she said and began stating facts that supported her point of view. She did not say anything negative about Carl and she did not brag about herself. She tried to speak briefly and stick with the facts.

"Maria has brought up some good points," the facilitator said. He moved on to the next agenda topic and Maria relaxed. She had not blown up but she had spoken up.

Asserting yourself without coming on too strong

Often we face unfair and biased situations. We have a right to feel angry, but we often harm ourselves when we express our raw emotions. Here are some of the tips Maria used to manage emotions and still be assertive:

- Take a moment to think things through.
- Notice which thoughts are pure fire and emotion. Set those aside and focus on facts.
- Select a calming phrase to repeat to yourself. Maria reminded herself, "It's not personal." Other phrases might be: "I am calm" and "I'm a good, clear communicator."
- Focus yourself and communicate directly, succinctly and clearly. Speak slowly and loudly enough so all can hear you.
- Use "I" statements; own the responsibility for what you are saying.
- Focus on the facts.
- Avoid saying anything negative about the other person.

Expressing emotions excellently

How do you act when you get angry or emotional? Do you blow up or clam up? Do you get in someone's face or storm out of the room? Do you silently stew and inwardly rant?

- Make a list of your emotional tendencies.
- What do you wish you could change about communicating when you're emotional?
- How can you take a step toward making those changes?
- How do you want someone to deal with you when you are emotional? Do you want questions, comfort or affirmation? Write down the ideal way to deal with you when you are upset, then use those ideas to soothe yourself as needed.

Conflict Quenchers

Relax your body and the mind will follow

When you're feeling angry, put yourself in a posture of openness and acceptance. Open your arms, soften your face and smile. Unclench your fists and be willing to look people in the eye. These simple physical gestures can help you relax and let go of anger and stress.

The power of silence

When angry words pulse through you, take a moment of silence. Visualize yourself as calm and happy, surrounded by people who appreciate and support you. Let yourself soak in those feelings before you speak.

In this chapter ...

You have learned how to understand and manage your emotions by:

C **Concentrating on the facts, rather than the emotions**

O **Opening yourself to opportunity for growth and learning**

N **Noticing how others view life**

F Forming new ways of looking at a situation

L **Learning deeper listening levels**

I Incorporating your priorities and values along with your analytical skills

C Connecting through problem solving

T Targeting solutions that invite creativity and build community

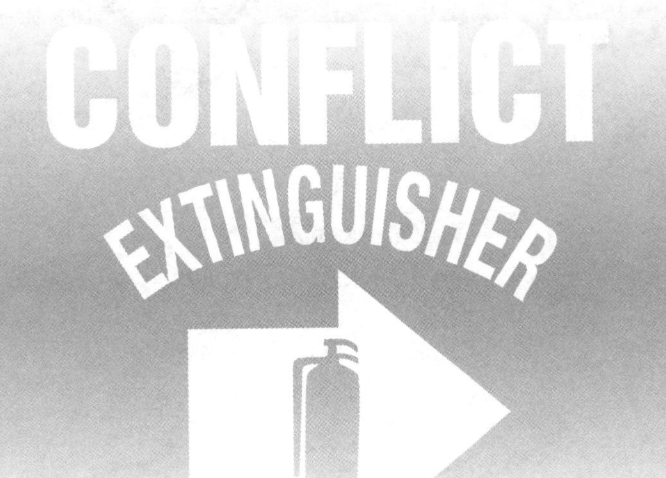

Chapter Nine

Feeding Your Skills: Learning Through Feedback

Linda did not do well at meetings. She had a naturally quiet manner and could easily fade into the background. When a co-worker made a snide or incorrect remark about her, Linda felt like sliding under the table and she acted as if she had. She did not correct the co-worker's information, but instead silently stewed. In Linda's workplace, the meek inherited the back seat and Linda's career was important to her. She wanted to be noticed, but not criticized. She hated sitting silently and not standing up for herself, but she was scared of conflict and honestly did not know how to act or what to say.

Angie also dreaded meetings. She could not keep her mouth shut. She had an opinion about everything and felt compelled to speak up. Conflict ignited and excited her and she knew she could argue with the best of them. But she recently had word from her supervisor to "tone it down" in meetings. Did he want her to turn into a blob of clay like Linda? Angie really did not know how to tone down without being totally silent.

Most of us have areas of communication that could be improved. Finding a friend or colleague to help you strengthen your conflict communication skills is a quick and easy way to enhance your confidence and broaden your abilities.

Selecting a conflict coach

Review the list of conflict communication areas that you'd like to improve. Think about the skills you want more of. Here are some examples:

- Brainstorming skills
- Active listening
- Clear communications
- Letting go of judgments
- Separating emotions from facts
- Creative problem solving

Think about the type of person who could best help you. If you are outspoken and quick to speak, you may want to work with someone calm. If you are shy and hate to defend or explain yourself, seek someone brimming with articulate confidence. Reach out to someone as a potential coach because:

- She has a conflict communications style you admire.
- She is a clear, kind and honest communicator and is a good, active listener.
- She seems like a fascinating and well-connected person and you'd like to get to know her better. Asking for advice can be a great way to increase your network while you learn.
- She attends many of the same meetings you do and has insight into the types of personalities you deal with.
- She knows you well and you feel sure she will be honest with you.
- You feel comfortable asking for help and/or offering to give help in return.

Coaching the coach: Describing the help you need

Once you select your potential coach, think about the kind of help you most want. Be clear in what you ask for. Suggest a small amount of time—for example, two hours a month. Then give her a chance to think about the offer.

Once you've followed up and she has agreed—of course, she will delighted to help you—discuss the kind of feedback and coaching she'll offer you. Here are some examples of the types of help you can ask for:

- Ask her to describe her outlook on conflict and to explain how she handles various conflict situations.
- Ask her how she learned to be so confident in her abilities. See if any of those tools apply to you.
- Get advice on a potential conflict in your life that is escalating.
- Brainstorm and strategize before you go into a conflict situation.
- Role-play various conflict scenarios, so you can practice the skills you want to improve.
- If she attends meetings with you, choose one meeting a month and have her critique your communication skills.
- If she attends other events with you, ask for feedback on any of your behaviors or communication that either reduce or build conflict.
- Ask for support. You might simply want encouragement and role-modeling. If she's in a meeting with you, you might want her to smile at you encouragingly and nod when you've tried a communication technique that is difficult for you.

Discuss the kind of feedback or critique you want. You want a critique style that you will listen to and absorb. When receiving feedback, you might want your coach to:

- State what you've done right. Ask her to be specific, telling you incidents, words, phrases or other communications that she felt really worked.
- State where she thinks you need improvements. To keep the critique concrete, ask her to state facts, then her observations. For example: "When I heard you telling Katlin that you wanted her report on your desk at nine, I thought your tone was abrupt and your body language was unfriendly."
- Give you concrete, "how-to" advice. For example: "Given Katlin's personality, I think a softer tone and more casual body language, such as standing with your arms open instead of crossed, might be more likely to reduce resentment and the potential for conflict."

Building your coaching corner

For shy Linda, asking Fran to coach her made a huge difference in her communication style. She asked Fran to model appropriate posture and body language across the table at meetings. She asked for non-verbal encouragement in meetings and for feedback after meetings.

Whenever Linda wanted to slump down and be invisible, she looked over at Fran, who was sitting straight and tall. One glance, and Linda literally straightened up. When Linda felt inclined to speak out, she glanced over at Fran, who nodded at her if she felt it was appropriate.

After the meeting, Fran praised Linda for her posture, and for some of the things she said. She pointed out other times where she could have spoken, or other ways she could have made her point more forcefully. Within a month of the coaching, Linda was no longer so afraid of conflict and her confidence had skyrocketed.

Think about your own needs and answer these questions:

Who are my potential coaches? List excellent communicators you feel comfortable approaching. Remember, you can have more than one coach.

1. ______________________________

2. ______________________________

3. ______________________________

4. ______________________________

What do I want from them? (For example: I want feedback on my behavior in meetings. I want a critique of how I present myself in conflict situations. I want advice on my body language.)

1. ______________________________

2. ______________________________

3. ______________________________

4. ______________________________

What kind of critique will I find most valuable? (Do you need praise? Do you need direct, no-nonsense communication?)

1. ______________________________

2. ______________________________

3. ______________________________

4. ______________________________

What results am I hoping for? (For example: A feeling of ease when others get angry or a feeling of confidence when I step into the middle of a conflict.)

1. ______________________________

2. ______________________________

3. ______________________________

4. ______________________________

Make a plan to approach your coach this week and ask for help. If one coach doesn't work out, try another.

While you are admiring someone's conflict management skills, she may be admiring yours! If someone asks you for coaching help, use the same questionnaire to find out what she needs. Coaching another person is a great way to increase your own skills.

Conflict Quenchers

Conflict to go

Hone your conflict communication skills at home as well as at the workplace. Notice how you respond to potential family conflict. Are you different when you're arguing with people you love? Do you like your home-based communications and behavior? Notice what areas you want to improve in the non-working parts of your life and seek coaching from friends and family as well. Homework can serve as valuable cross-training for work-related situations.

What's underneath?

Go beyond the slings and arrows of outrageous conflict and try to understand the motivation and hidden meanings, both of yourself and of others. What makes you want to slide under the table or shake your fist in a face? What makes others shout or sulk? You'll enjoy trying to figure out the inner workings of others. Having a deeper understanding of people's behaviors can help you feel more at ease.

In this chapter . . .

You've learned how to get yourself support and coaching by:

C Concentrating on the facts, rather than the emotions

O **Opening yourself to opportunity for growth and learning**

N **Noticing how others view life**

F Forming new ways of looking at a situation

L **Learning deeper listening levels**

I Incorporating your priorities and values along with your analytical skills

C **Connecting through problem solving**

T Targeting solutions that invite creativity and build community

Summary

You have now explored and worked through the major components of honing your own personal skills. I hope you will continue to study and use the principles and methods of the six acronyms designed to give you a sense of confidence, self-esteem and calm when the next conflict comes your way.

C Concentrate on the facts, not the emotions

O Open yourself to opportunity for growth and learning

N Notice how others view life

F Form new ways of looking at a situation

L Learn deeper listening levels

I Incorporate your priorities and values along with your analytical skills

C Connect through problem-solving

T Target solutions that invite creativity and build community

---

S Solo

T Topic

I Intention

L Length of meeting

L Location and time

T Think through the meeting in advance
H Hear what the person has to say
E Echo back what you heard
R Relate your own side of the story
E Encourage the person to repeat back to you

R Review the facts
E Eliminate the emotions
S See both sides of the story
T Think about commonality

C Create notes that cover the important points
H Help yourself stay centered
I Invite the contentious person to speak first
L Let the contentious person be first to offer solutions
L Leave emotions out of it and stay focused on common goals

C Create a list of the issues and events bothering you
A Acknowledge the facts and your feelings
L Leave time for your stress-soothers
M Manage to express yourself appropriately